EVERYTHING I NEED TO KNOW ABOUT ELECTRICITY
...WELL ALMOST

GORDON KLIMENKO

ILLUSTRATED BY: **JUSTIN CURRIE**

AN INTRODUCTION TO THE SCIENCE AND ENGINEERING OF ELECTRICITY IN THE DIGITAL INFORMATION AGE

© 2011 Gordon Klimenko

All rights reserved. No part of this work may be reproduced or transmitted in any form or by any means, electronic or mechanical, including photocopying and recording, or by any information storage and retrieval system without permission in writing from the author.

Manufactured by Friesens Corporation; Altona, Manitoba, Canada; September 2011; Job # 67123

Library and Archives Canada Cataloguing in Publication

Klimenko, Gordon A. (Gordon Anthony), 1954-
Everything I need to know about electricity --well almost : an introduction to the science and engineering of electricity in the digital information age
          /Gordon Klimenko ; illustrated by Justin Currie.

Includes index.
ISBN 978-0-9876885-0-7

1. Electricity--Juvenile literature.
2. Electrons--Juvenile literature.
3. Computers--Juvenile literature.
4. Digital electronics--Juvenile literature.
5. Chemistry--Juvenile literature.
6. Physics--Juvenile literature.

I. Currie, Justin, 1986- II. Title.

QC527.2.K55 2011 j537 C2011-904687-3

Photo Credits: NASA, iStock, Aimin Song, Daniel Pihan and Steve Mann
All photos and images used with permission.

Printed in Canada, September 2011

EverythingIneedtoknow.org

To my boys, Martin and Marko and all young people like them…

Acknowledgements

To my friend and mentor, Witold Kinsner, Professor of Electrical and Computer Engineering, University of Manitoba, who helped me understand through all these years.

To Géneviève Degraves, Jeff Pospishell, Gary Isleifson, Jim Martin, Mark Alexiuk, Terry Bilyk, Bev Phillips, Jordan and James Currie and my sons who helped proof my work.

To Steve Mann for the Chapter 4 title page depicting his daughter connecting a garden hose to a Hydralophone (water-pipe-organ-flute). http://funtain.ca/

And to Rachel, our cartoon mascot who has helped develop, teach and explore the sciences of electricity in a new and fun way.

To NASA, PBS's NOVA, CBC's Quirks & Quarks, Discovery's Daily Planet, and to Manitoba Hydro's Electrical Museum who have gone out of their way to inspire and teach.

and to Wikipedia, for giving the world a starting point for everything

Preface

As an engineer and father I was surprised when looking through my son's Grade 6 Science book to see the same material introducing the topic of electricity that I saw when I was in Grade 6 back in the 1960s. It showed the basics of static charge like a balloon sticking to a wall and pictures of light bulbs and conventional wall light switches.

Today, in the 21st century, we live in a different world. The advent of the microchip and computers made teaching the subject of electricity much more relevant and fascinating.

My career has taken me along some amazing journeys and has allowed me to see things that I thought incomprehensible clearly in a different way.

I wanted to share what I know with my sons in such a way that any entry level or high school student can grasp. The concepts laid here are not complicated. All one needs is imagination. The heart of the digital information age involving computers, the Internet, smart phones, jump drives, music, video and cameras are explored through a young girl named Rachel. All this is explained in a non-technical, pragmatic way through a strongly visual picture book format.

I am hoping that this work, in some way, will spark further interest and study in Science and Engineering. I can tell you, it is one heck of a ride, and … it's just beginning!

About the Author: Gordon Klimenko

While Gord completed his undergraduate degree in Mechanical Engineering, he was fascinated by the beauty, power and value of the i8080 & Z80 microchips, which led him to complete a graduate studies degree in Electrical and Computer Engineering at the University of Manitoba. The first half of his career was with Lockheed Martin and he is now Director of R&D Engineering Innovation at IMRIS Inc., focusing on image guided surgical imaging solutions. Both companies are located in Winnipeg, Canada, where he currently resides. He loves doing his own home renovations and is a Mopar car enthusiast.

Contact: Gord@everythingineedtoknow.org

About the Artist: Justin Currie

Justin grew up on a farm outside the small town of La Riviere, Manitoba. Growing up with art and drawing as a large part of his life, it seemed only natural that he further his education in an art-related field, including design and print production. Justin currently resides in Winnipeg, working in a video game studio and continues to draw on every scrap of paper he gets a hold of.

Website: www.currieart.blogspot.com
Contact: Justin@everythingineedtoknow.org

About Rachel

Rachel is a young, curious student, passionate about our planet and its preservation. She's confident the only way to do this is with creative, innovative thinking, and thirst for knowledge.

She also has a passion for sushi – especially from Ta.Ke Sushi.

Contact: Rachel@everythingineedtoknow.org

TABLE OF CONTENTS

Chapter 1: Learning about water flow helps me understand electricity. **8**

Chapter 2: What is an electron? **18**

Chapter 3: Computers are built from tiny switches called transistors. **42**

Chapter 4: What does digital mean? **54**

Chapter 5: A different view of time **66**

Closing Remarks **70**

Chapter 1:
Learning about water flow helps me understand electricity

Everything *I* Need To Know About Electricity

Electricity is all about the flow of electrons and can be very dangerous to you. It should <u>never</u> be played with.

If you ever see sparks coming from an electronic device, shut it off and go get help!

On the other hand, the flow of water out of a garden hose can be safe and fun to play with.

Even at a very young age, Rachel can understand water pressure and flow out of a garden hose.

9

Learning about water flow helps me understand electricity

A Super Soaker* can teach me a lot about electricity

When talking about either WATER or ELECTRICITY, the concepts of FLOW RATE and PRESSURE are the same.

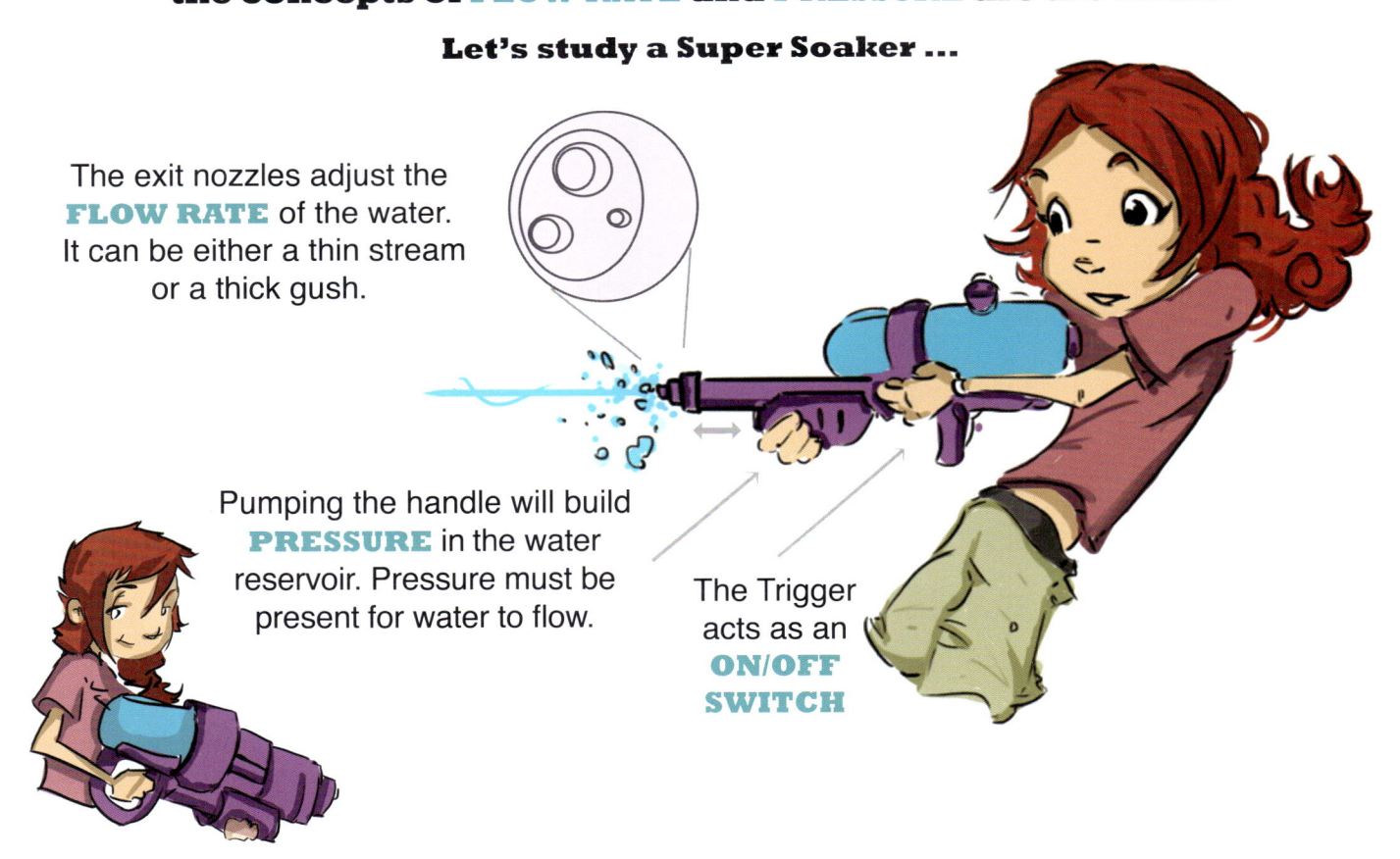

Let's study a Super Soaker ...

The exit nozzles adjust the **FLOW RATE** of the water. It can be either a thin stream or a thick gush.

Pumping the handle will build **PRESSURE** in the water reservoir. Pressure must be present for water to flow.

The Trigger acts as an **ON/OFF SWITCH**

In electricity the electron FLOW RATE is called CURRENT and electron PRESSURE is called VOLTAGE. The trigger is an ON/OFF SWITCH called a TRANSISTOR.

*Super Soaker is property of Hasbro

10

Everything *I* Need To Know About Electricity

How does water teach me about electricity?

WATER

FLOW RATE
With water, flow rate is a measurement of the amount or volume of water moving per unit time. For example, the flow rate of a garden hose can be measured in gallons per minute or litres per second.

PRESSURE
Water pressure is "force per unit area" and can be viewed as the "desire to move". Water will not flow unless there is pressure. It is measured in psi (lbs/in^2) or bar. Water will not flow out of a Super Soaker unless you pump or pressurize the reservoir.

HOSE LENGTH
If you have a very, very long hose, or the inside surface of the hose is rough, water has a difficult time pushing through. The surface opposes or resists the flow.
Water always follows the path of least resistance.

TAP or FAUCET
A tap, faucet or valve is an on/off switch that controls the flow of water.

ELECTRICITY

CURRENT
The flow rate of electrons is called current and is measured in coulombs per second or amps. One amp has a flow rate of 6 million trillion (10^{18}) electrons per second. A toaster uses ~10 amps, a light bulb ~1/2 amp.

VOLTAGE
Electron pressure is similar and can be viewed as the "desire to move". Electron pressure or potential difference is called voltage and is measured in volts. If there is no difference in voltage between two ends of a wire, no electrons will flow.

RESISTANCE
If you have a very, very long wire, or the wire is a poor conductor, electrons have a difficult time travelling through. This poses an opposition to electron flow.
Electrons always follow the path of least resistance.

TRANSISTOR
A transistor is an on/off switch, similar to a light switch at home, that controls the flow of electrons.

Learning about water flow helps me understand electricity

Electricity Basics

Electricity describes the behaviour of electrons and their relationship between positive (+) and negative (-) charges.

- **Electricity** flowing in a wire describes the movement of a huge number of incredibly small bits of energy called electrons. They are invisible to the naked eye because they are very small and move very fast. This may be hard to understand.

Van de Graaff generators show the basics of electrostatic charge. The ancient Greeks discovered that if you rubbed amber (petrified tree sap) with rabbit fur, it could pick up straw magically through the air. The Greek name for amber is ... ELECTRON!

200 years ago, a German high school teacher, *Georg Ohm,* defined the relationship between electron flow, pressure and resistance.

Ohm's Law

V= Voltage (volts): $V = I \times R$
I= Current (amps): $I = V \div R$
R= Resistance (ohms): $R = V \div I$

P= Power (watts): $P = V \times I$
(e.g., a 60 watt light bulb = 120 volts x 1/2 amp)

Everything *I* Need To Know About Electricity

Resistance

- A garden hose will lose pressure over a very long distance due to the resistance it must overcome pushing the water through the hose. Similarly, voltage will be lost over a very long distance due to the resistance it must overcome pushing the electrons through the wire.

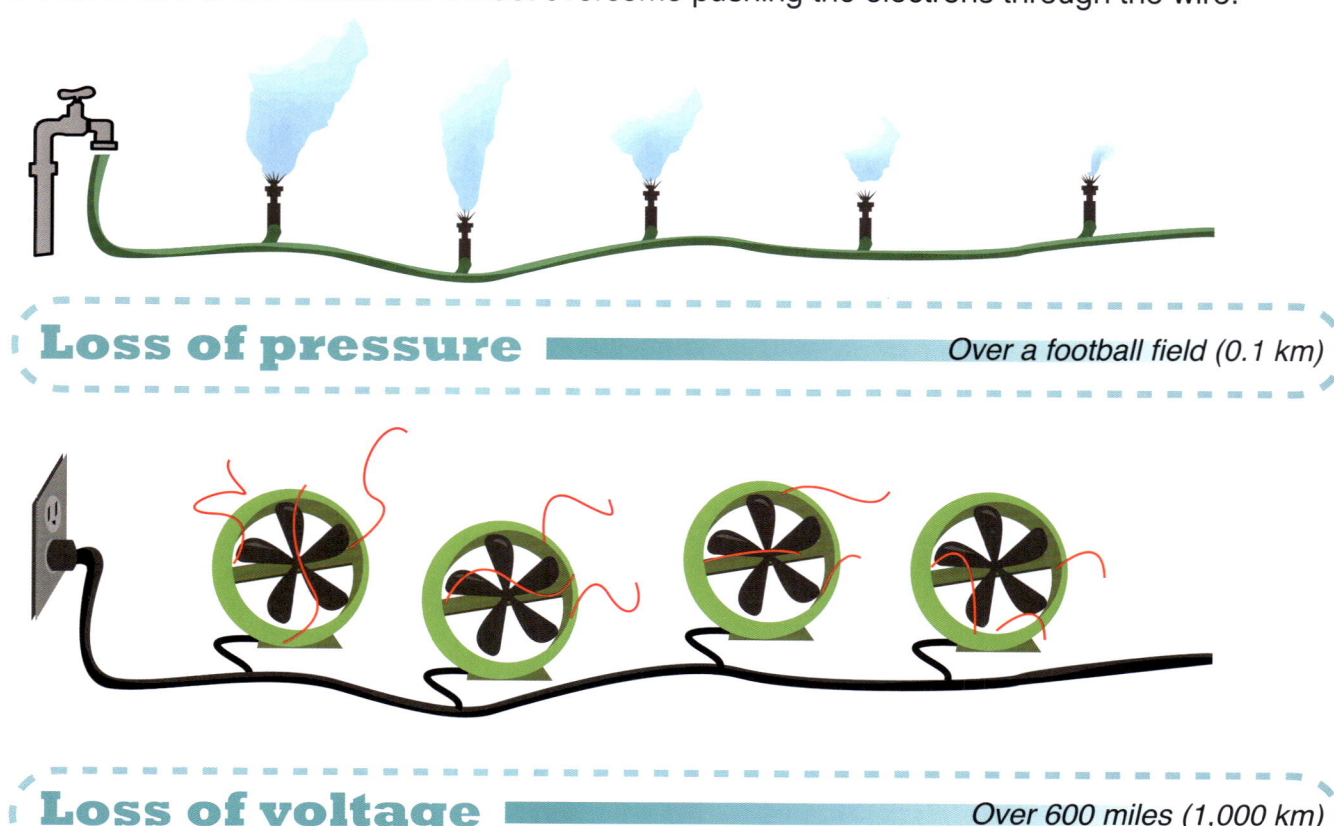

Loss of pressure — *Over a football field (0.1 km)*

Loss of voltage — *Over 600 miles (1,000 km)*

- Comparing electricity with water, the distance of scale is very different. With water, you will see the above pressure loss over 0.1 km. With electricity, power from 1,000 km away will experience voltage loss as a result of resistive transmission line losses. Electrons normally would travel at the speed of light, however, they slow down by 20% to ~500 million miles per hour when travelling through wire due to the resistance they must overcome.

13

Learning about water flow helps me understand electricity

Do it yourself at home: How to understand water FLOW RATE

1) Put an empty measuring cup under your kitchen sink faucet.

2) Turn the water on and let it flow slowly. Look at a clock and time the event for 10 seconds.

3) Divide the volume of water collected in the measuring cup by 10 and you have the FLOW RATE (e.g. litres per second).

How to understand water PRESSURE

Stick your finger under the faucet and see how far the spray of water shoots. The higher the pressure, the further it shoots.
(Maybe it's best to try this in your bathtub.)

A Super Soaker Trigger is an On/Off Switch

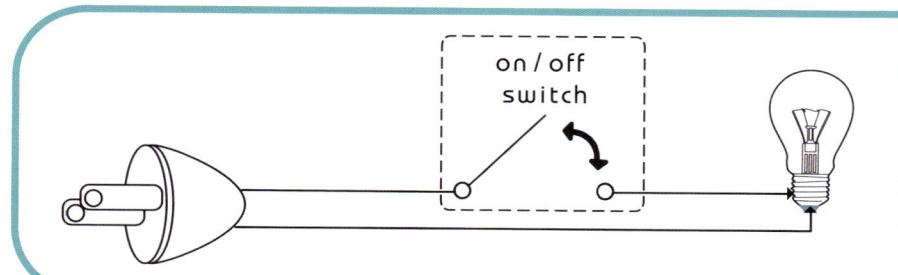

Inside an incandescent light bulb a tungsten filament gets heated, causing electrons to move, and emits photons, or light.

A typical light bulb (60 watt) has 3 million trillion (10^{18}) electrons flowing through it every second.

- All computers are made from millions of transistors which are nothing more than tiny electrical ON/OFF switches. They are connected together by incredibly small wires. Similarly, a water tap, faucet or Super Soaker trigger are all ON/OFF switches.

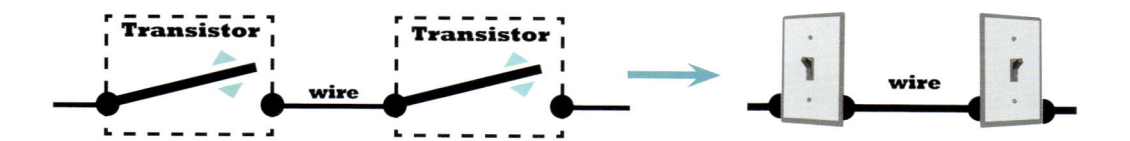

How can 3 million trillion electrons per second travelling at 500 million miles per hour flow through that?

15

Learning about water flow helps me understand electricity

Knowing about water helps me understand how a digital computer works…

Compare a piece of wire between 2 transistors to a length of garden hose between 2 taps. Both taps and transistors act as **ON / OFF** switches. If you hold the hose in your hands and turn on the wall tap you will feel the hose get **HARD** because water pressure is present. If you shut off the wall tap the hose remains hard. If you press the spray nozzle hose tap, a squirt of water will discharge and the hose will get **SOFT** because no water pressure is present. This same concept applies to electron pressure called voltage flowing into a wire separated by transistors.

All digital computers work similarly.

- **Depending** on which transistor is on or off, the wire can have:
  - a voltage present, FULL of electron pressure, or
  - no voltage present, EMPTY of electron pressure.

- **This is the definition** of a digital state, or "BIT". It has a state of full or empty. In computer lingo, instead of saying "full" or "empty", we refer to the state as "1" or "0".

Electron Pressure Present
Digital 1

Electron Pressure Absent
Digital 0

16

Everything I Need To Know About Electricity

...It's all about containing pressure!

HOSE HARD
HIGH PRESSURE

If you bend or kink a hose, pressure builds and the hose gets hard in your hand.

**Same as
Electron Pressure Present
Digital 1**

HOSE SOFT
LOW PRESSURE

When you un-kink the hose, the built-up pressure will discharge and the hose gets soft in your hand.

**Same as
Electron Pressure Absent
Digital 0**

Chapter 2:
What is an electron?

- **An electron is an incredibly small bit of negatively charged energy that exists around the positively charged nucleus of an atom.**

- **The atom** is the fundamental building block of all matter in the universe. The interaction of negatively charged electrons define all matter around us. Everything, and I mean everything, is made up of atoms.

- **Atoms are studied in the 3 main branches of science:**
  - **CHEMISTRY** is the science of elements, their behaviour, how they react, and the way they combine to form compounds that exist everywhere around us.
  - **PHYSICS** is the science concerned with the study of properties and interactions of space, time, matter and energy and gravity. This includes the study of the very large (planets) as well as the very small (atoms).
  - **BIOLOGY** is the science of living organisms.
    atoms ➢ molecules ➢ cells ➢ tissues ➢ organs ➢ organisms

Traditional (Bohr) model of an atom

- Every **atom** or **element** known (so far) is listed on a chart called the Periodic Table.

- **Six Million Trillion (10^{18})** electrons are needed to give 1 amp (or coulomb per second) of charge!

- **An electron** was first defined over 100 years ago in 1895 by James Thompson.

- Traditionally, an electron orbiting its nucleus was compared to the moon orbiting the Earth or the planets orbiting the Sun. **Well ... there is much more!**

19

What is an electron?

Size of an Atom

- **The atom** is very small and mostly space. Ten million atoms lined up in a row would equal 1 mm. The outer orbit of the electron is 100,000 times that of the diameter of the nucleus. The electron can be very, very far away from the nucleus. Up until recently, this empty space was called the "ether".

- **The centre** nucleus of an atom weighs 1,835 times more than an electron.

- When atoms combine they form molecules or compounds. If you had a beaker of water containing precisely 18 ml water (H_2O) you would have exactly 1 mole or 0.602 trillion trillion (6.02×10^{23}) molecules of water.

- **An electron** weighs 9.1×10^{-31} kilogram or 10 millionths of a trillionth of a trillionth of a kilogram.

- **The electron** does not have a defined orbit like the planets or moon. It exists on a cloud or atmosphere, which has a defined shape and it exists everywhere on the surface of that shape.

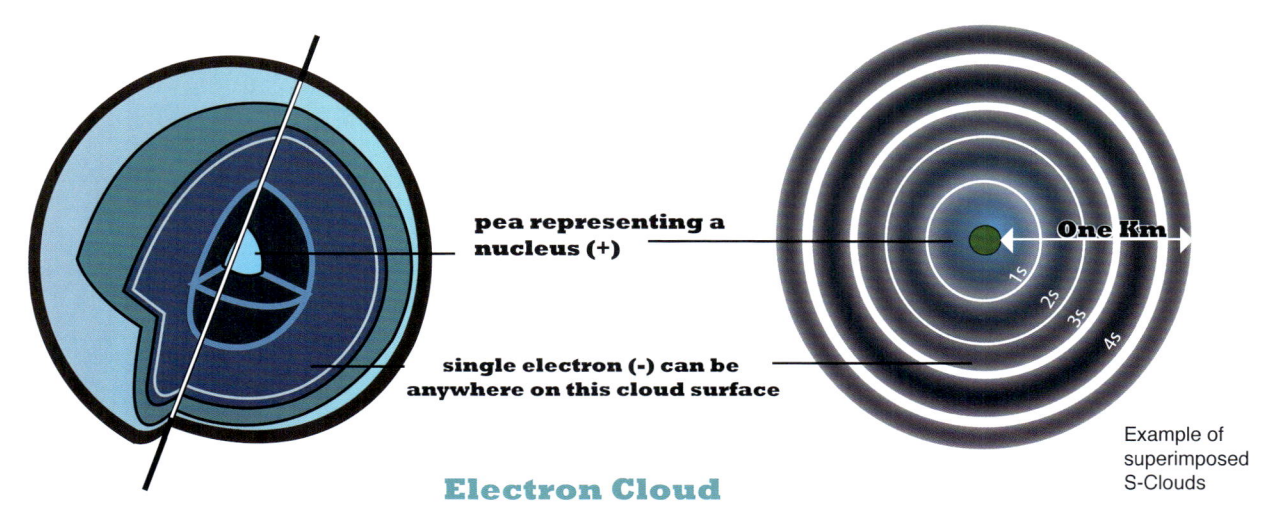

pea representing a nucleus (+)

single electron (-) can be anywhere on this cloud surface

Electron Cloud

One Km

1s 2s 3s 4s

Example of superimposed S-Clouds

20

Everything *I* Need To Know About Electricity

Electron Distance from its Nucleus

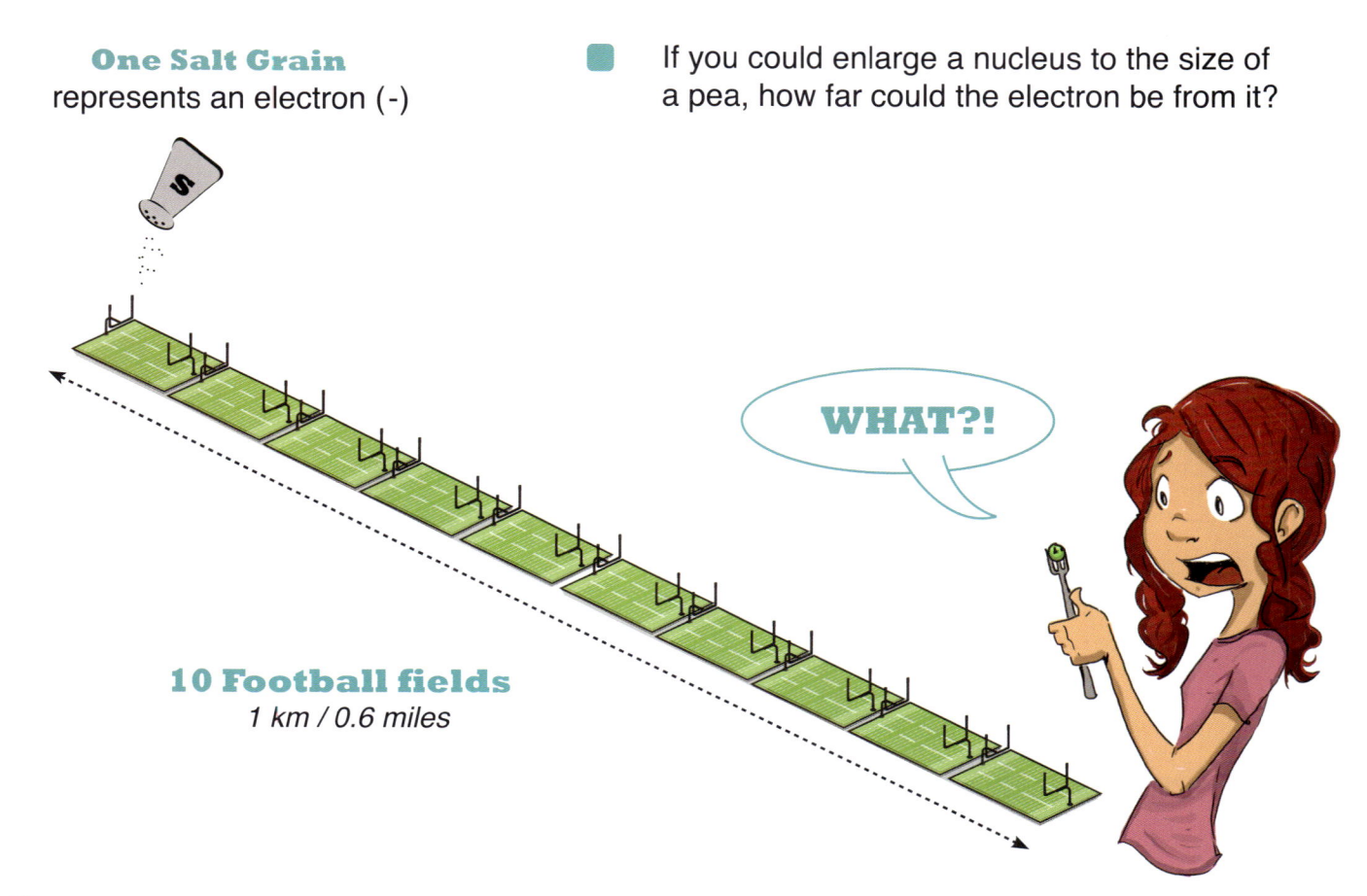

One Salt Grain represents an electron (-)

If you could enlarge a nucleus to the size of a pea, how far could the electron be from it?

10 Football fields
1 km / 0.6 miles

WHAT?!

Next time you are having dinner, imagine a pea representing a nucleus and a grain of salt an electron. Take this grain of salt and place it 10 football fields away. This is a similar scale you could see within an atom.

Pea represents a nucleus (+)

What is an electron?

Electron Cloud Shapes

- **The clouds** in the sky have different shapes and **NATURE** does the same with electrons.

- Negatively charged electrons exist around the positively charged nucleus of an atom and occupy different energy levels. Each energy level has a different physical appearance. They are often referred to as clouds or atmospheres.

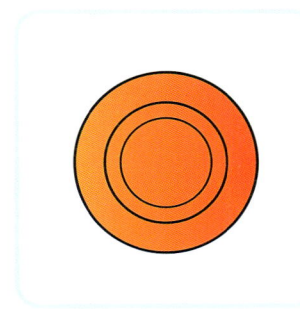

S-electron cloud

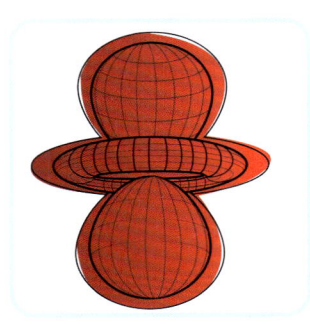

D-electron cloud
This is an example of one of 5 D-clouds.
It is by far the coolest!

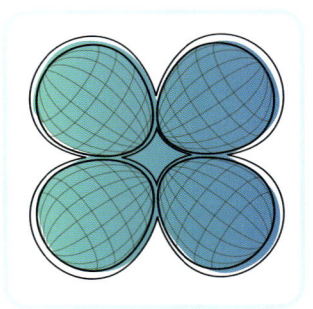

P-electron cloud
This is an example of 2 of 3 P-clouds.

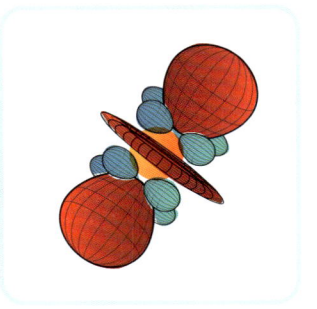

Depending on the atom, all orbitals could be present. The nucleus is hidden inside.

These are what atoms really look like!
NATURE IS ALWAYS BEAUTIFUL

- There are many other interesting cloud shapes. Think of them as peculiarly shaped atmospheres around a nucleus. Here are 3 of 7 F-cloud shapes.

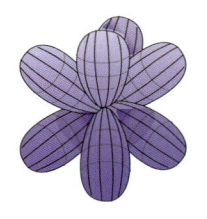

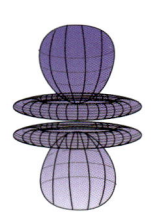

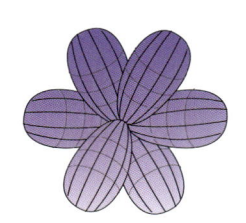

Everything *I* Need To Know About Electricity

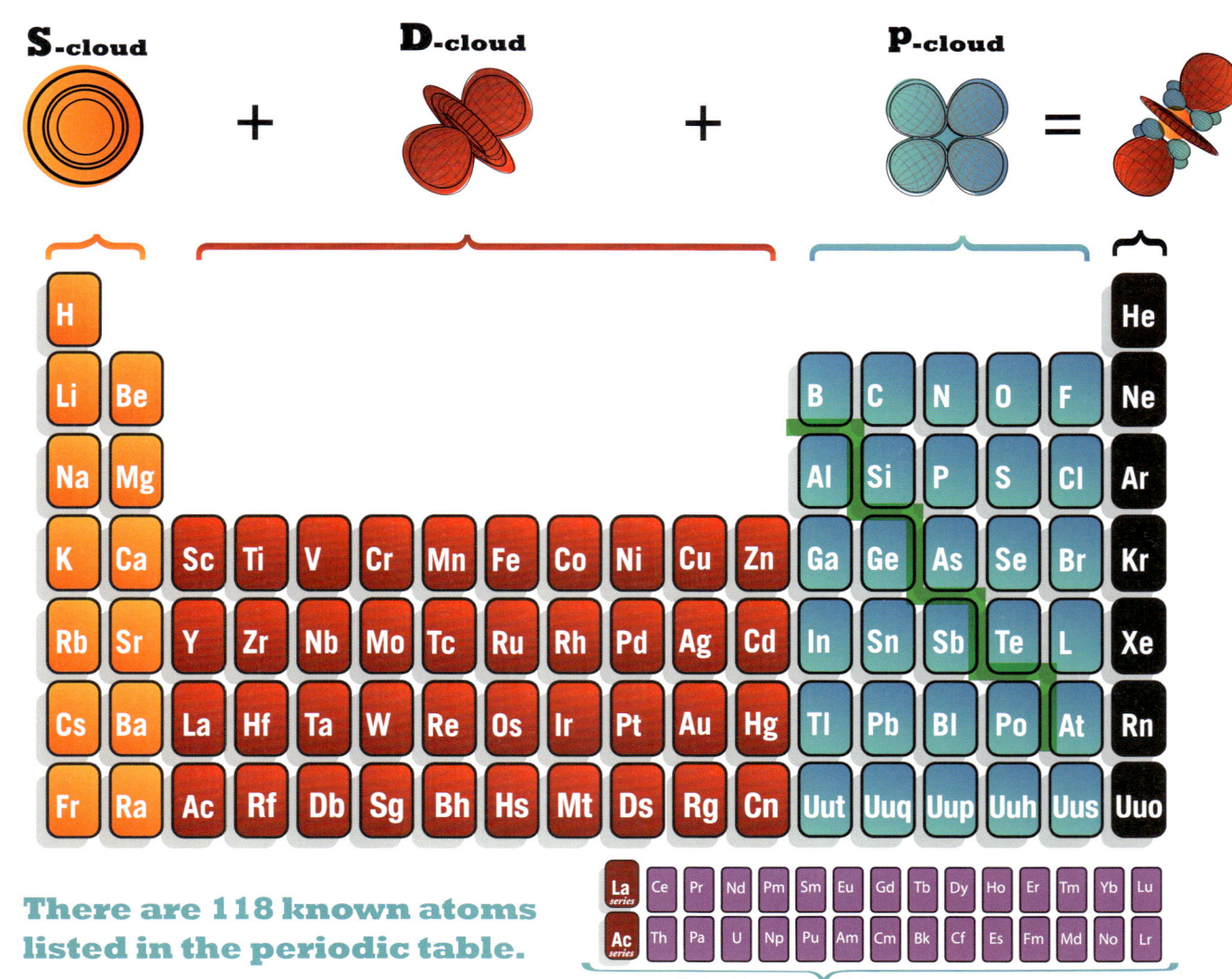

S-cloud + **D-cloud** + **P-cloud** =

H																	He
Li	Be											B	C	N	O	F	Ne
Na	Mg											Al	Si	P	S	Cl	Ar
K	Ca	Sc	Ti	V	Cr	Mn	Fe	Co	Ni	Cu	Zn	Ga	Ge	As	Se	Br	Kr
Rb	Sr	Y	Zr	Nb	Mo	Tc	Ru	Rh	Pd	Ag	Cd	In	Sn	Sb	Te	L	Xe
Cs	Ba	La	Hf	Ta	W	Re	Os	Ir	Pt	Au	Hg	Tl	Pb	Bl	Po	At	Rn
Fr	Ra	Ac	Rf	Db	Sg	Bh	Hs	Mt	Ds	Rg	Cn	Uut	Uuq	Uup	Uuh	Uus	Uuo

| La series | Ce | Pr | Nd | Pm | Sm | Eu | Gd | Tb | Dy | Ho | Er | Tm | Yb | Lu |
| Ac series | Th | Pa | U | Np | Pu | Am | Cm | Bk | Cf | Es | Fm | Md | No | Lr |

F-cloud (not discussed; many are man-made)

There are 118 known atoms listed in the periodic table.

- Groups of elements with the same electron cloud shapes are grouped together to form the periodic table.

- There is a maximum number of electrons each cloud can hold. The S-cloud can hold up to 2 electrons, P-cloud 6, D-cloud 10 and the F-cloud 14.

23

What is an electron?

When electrons exist in a cloud or atmosphere, what does that mean?

- Imagine sitting in a room, listening to music. You can hear the music everywhere in the room no matter where you are.

- The reason you can hear the music everywhere in the room is that a WAVE is transmitting the acoustic energy (changes in air pressure) in all directions, which we call music to our ears. Waves are everywhere. Cell phones work because of electromagnetic waves. Talking and listening are possible because of waves. Wind occurs as a result of waves and of course we all know water waves.

- Imagine the speaker is the nucleus of an atom, the music is the electron and the room is the cloud shape. **THIS IS WHAT AN ELECTRON IS:** A spherical standing wave of energy around the nucleus of an atom.

Energy or sound exists everywhere in the room!

Everything I Need To Know About Electricity

Electrons are Spherical Standing Energy Waves

The patterns seen from electron waves would be similar to the patterns seen in water, except they are spherical!

An electron's standing wave could be viewed as a pure tone produced by a tuning fork except that it never fades away. Inside an atom, this energy is always present.

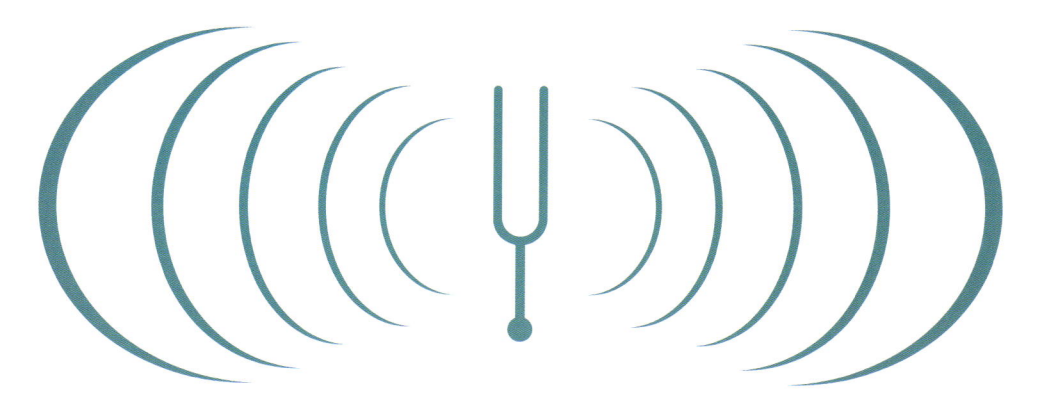

Did you know ... If you hit a single tuning fork in a room filled with other identical tuning forks, they will ALL start to vibrate.

Particle-Wave Duality:
Electrons Act as Both Particles and Waves

When you fire a small number of electrons (say 10) at an electron detector through two slits, they show up on the detector as individual specks. This would make you think that the electron is a particle. If you fire a large number (say 10,000) of electrons at the same two slits, you would expect these specks to pile up under these two slits.

BUT THIS DOES NOT HAPPEN

Electrons still show up as individual specks on the detector as if they were particles but they are concentrated in a striped pattern as if they were waves.
This is what James Thompson discovered in 1895!

Everything *I* Need To Know About Electricity

Where have we seen this stripe pattern before?

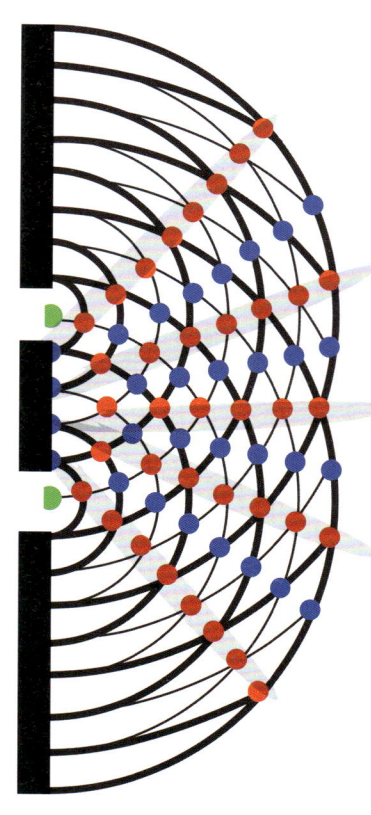

courtesy of Daniel Pihan

If a single wave hits two slits the resulting wave interference will show up as a striped pattern.

It's beautiful how nature repeats itself time and time again.

27

What is an electron?

Electrons can be Focused into a Beam and Steered by a Magnetic Field

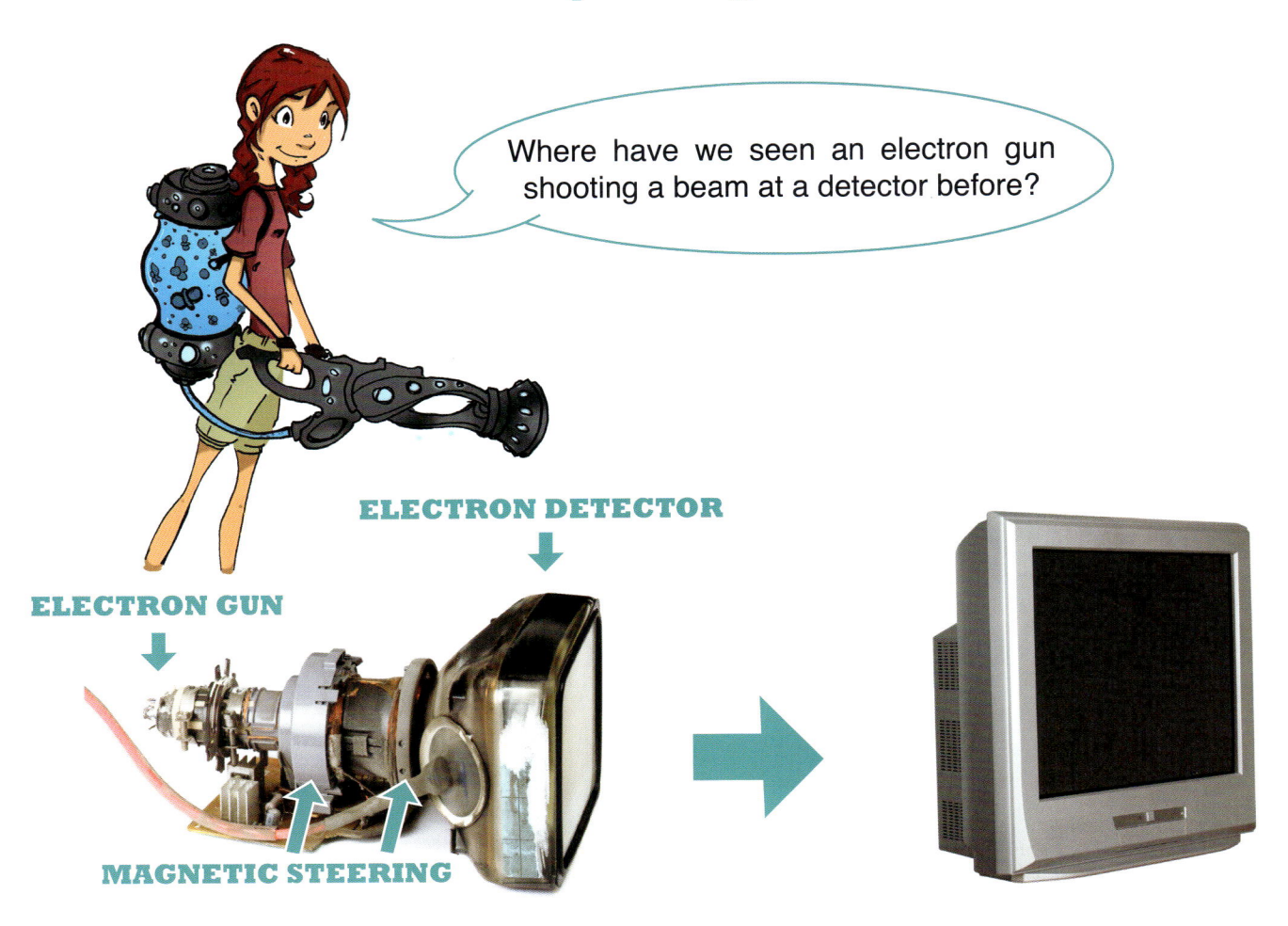

Where have we seen an electron gun shooting a beam at a detector before?

ELECTRON DETECTOR

ELECTRON GUN

MAGNETIC STEERING

Old-style TVs and computer monitors use the same principle and were called **cathode ray tubes (CRTs)**. Newer flat panel **LCD** and **plasma** televisions do not use an electron gun. They use digitally addressable pixels to display the video.

Everything I Need To Know About Electricity

- At a billionth (10^{-9}) of a metre scale, we see an electron wave moving through a narrow constriction at 6 consecutive moments in time totalling 2.3 trillionths of a second.

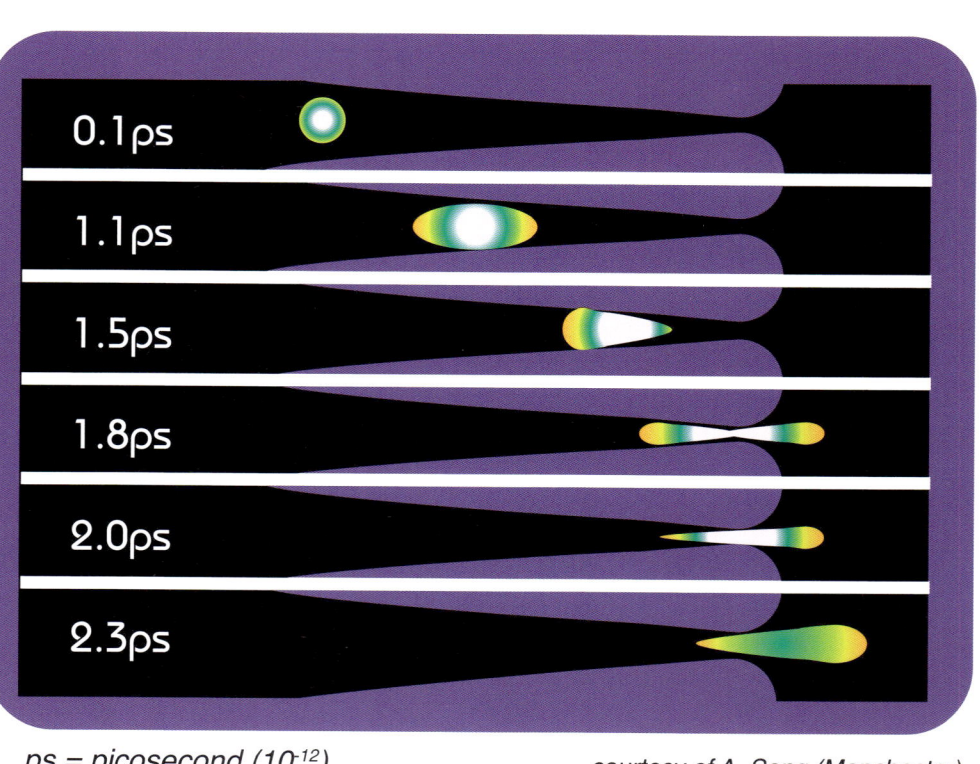

Kind of like a balloon but it is energy

0.1ρs
1.1ρs
1.5ρs
1.8ρs
2.0ρs
2.3ρs

ps = picosecond (10^{-12})

courtesy of A. Song (Manchester)

MATTER AND ENERGY ARE THE SAME!

What is an electron?

Conductors, Insulators and Semiconductors

- **Electrons are spherical standing waves of energy** around the nucleus of an atom that can exist in various cloud shapes. They are negatively charged and are repelled by neighbouring negatively charged electrons while being attracted to the nucleus's positively charged proton.

- **Cloud shapes represent specific energy levels!** The gap between these energy levels define whether the atom is an insulator or conductor, with semiconductors somewhere in between.

- Electrons can only exist in specific energy levels around an atom. Think of the steps on a staircase...You can only stand on a specific stair. **You can not be standing in between stairs.** Similarly, electrons can only exist in specific energy levels or bands and can be viewed as orbitals.

- **These orbitals or energy bands** exist around all atoms whether they have electrons in them or not... And they can be very far away from the atom's nucleus... These bands prevent the negatively charged electrons from spiralling into the positively charged nucleus.

Ever played with stacking dolls?
Electrons exist similarly on the surface of stacking clouds!

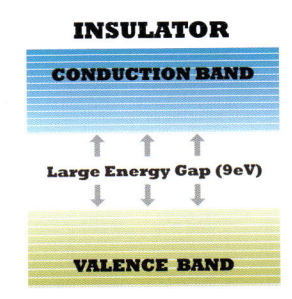

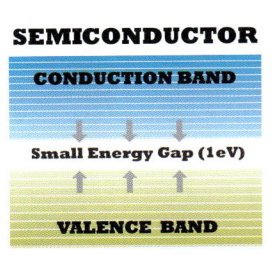

INSULATOR
CONDUCTION BAND
Large Energy Gap (9eV)
VALENCE BAND

SEMICONDUCTOR
CONDUCTION BAND
Small Energy Gap (1eV)
VALENCE BAND

CONDUCTOR
CONDUCTION BAND
VALENCE BAND

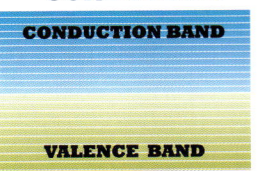

eV = electron Volt

Everything *I* Need To Know About Electricity

conductors ← | → **insulators**

GET YOUR FREE ELECTRONS HERE!

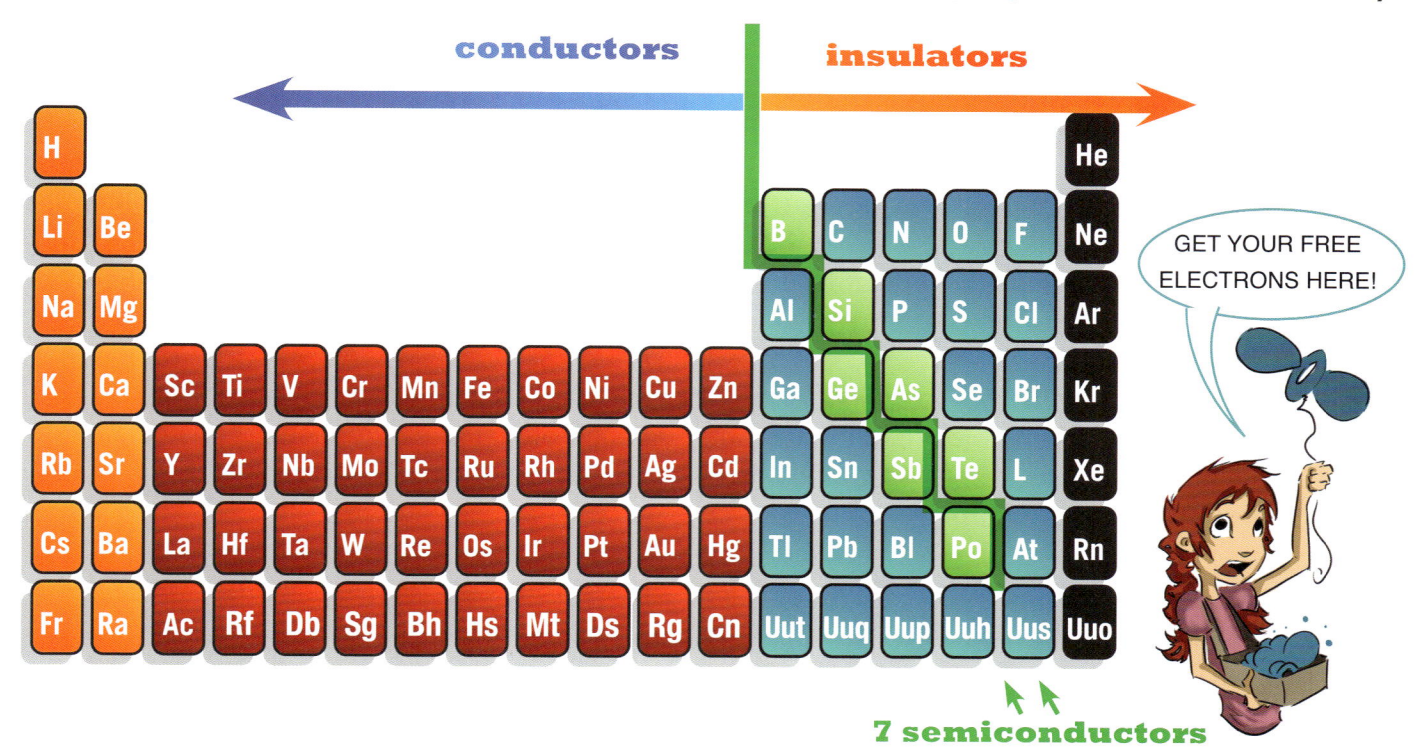

7 semiconductors

- **CONDUCTORS** readily release their outermost electrons. In a conductor, a free electron is one that is not bound or tied to a specific atom. It is free to wander around between atoms. In a metal which is a good conductor, there are approximately 10 billion trillion (10^{22}) free electrons per cm^3 (size of a sugar cube) wandering around. A small amount of voltage (electron pressure) present will cause these electrons to move.

- **INSULATORS** readily accept or share additional electrons. In an insulator, there are almost no free electrons. In a good insulator, there are approximately 10 free electrons per cm^3 wandering around. The rest are all held tightly bound to the atoms. Even with a voltage present, these electrons will not move.

- The elements that overlap and border **CONDUCTORS** and **INSULATORS** are called **SEMICONDUCTORS** and can be made to behave both as conductors and insulators.

31

What is an electron?

Happiness is a Filled Outer Valence Orbital

Atoms in the **outer right column** of the periodic table have a FULL outer valence orbital or cloud shape. These are called INERT or NOBLE since they can not join with anything. These atoms are in EQUILIBRIUM and could be considered "happy".

The rest of the periodic table contains atoms with either extra electrons or missing electrons in their outer valence orbital or cloud shape. They will try to mate or bond together with other atoms forming molecules in order to attain equilibrium and be happy.

- For electricity to flow, there must be a lot of **FREE ELECTRONS** available.

- Atoms in good conductors such as copper, gold or silver have only a single electron in their outermost valence orbital. It is all alone out there and is very far away from its positively charged nucleus. It is also surrounded by packed orbitals full of neighbouring negatively charged electrons.

COPPER HAS AN ELECTRON CONFIGURATION OF
$1S^2\ 2S^2\ 2P^6\ 3S^2\ 3P^6\ 3D^{10}$ $4S^1$

Filled inner orbitals   **Single electron in unfilled outer orbital**

- The neighbouring negatively charged electrons insulate the attractive force of the positively charged nucleus and want to repel this lonely $4S^1$ electron. Therefore, it is bound to the nucleus very weakly.

- In a **SEMICONDUCTOR** the number of free electrons lies somewhere in between. Here, the valence electrons are not free to wander around as they are in a metal, but are trapped in a bond between adjacent atoms.

Atom Glue

There are 3 primary ways atoms can BOND or GLUE together to form molecules or compounds:

- ### IONIC BONDING
  Ionic bonding is a result of a joining together of positive and negative ions. For example, sodium is a positive ion since it has an extra electron in its S orbital – it's written as Na^{+1}. Chlorine is a negative ion since it is short an electron in its P orbital – it's written as Cl^{-1}. The two ions bond together to form NaCl (sodium chloride) – ordinary table salt.

- ### COVALENT BONDING
  Covalent bonding involves the sharing of electrons between specific atoms. Atoms always try to form a FULL outer valence orbital. For example, oxygen ($1S^2$, $2S^2$, $2P^4$) has only 4 out of 6 electrons in its outer 2P orbital. It will bond with 2 hydrogen atoms, with each having only one electron ($1S^1$). These 3 atoms share a covalent bond to form H_2O – water.

- ### METALLIC BONDING
  Metallic bonding also involves the sharing of electrons but they are not between specific atoms. They establish equilibrium by sharing electrons from a pool or sea of electrons. The outer valence electrons are free to wander between the atoms. They no longer belong to a single atom.

- ### All bonding is a result of interaction of the outermost valence electrons.

Remember, all atoms want to be happy!… So do we!

What is an electron?

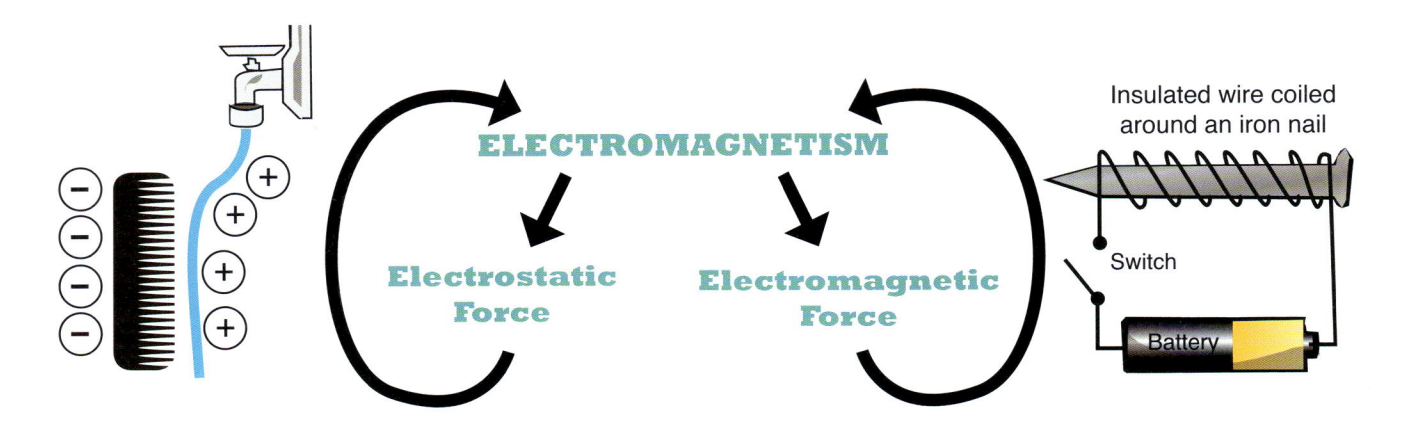

- Electromagnetism is comprised of two forces, the electromagnetic force and the electrostatic force.

- If you run a comb through your hair several times and hold it above small cut up pieces of paper, the paper will be attracted to the comb. Similarly, if you place this comb beside a thin stream of water, the stream will bend. This movement is caused by a force called the **electrostatic force.**

- When electrons flow, an invisible magnetic field forms at 90 degrees to the current flow. By turning a lamp on or off, you will see a compass needle react to the magnetic field. Similarly if you wrap an iron nail with an insulated wire and attach a battery, you will create a simple **electromagnet** that could pick up paper clips. This movement is caused by a force called the **electromagnetic force**.

- **Electron Reciprocity:**
  - A changing electron flow will always result in a changing magnetic field.
  - A changing magnetic field will always produce a changing electron flow.

- **ELECTROMAGNETISM** describes both static electricity and magnetism.

THEY ARE NOT DIFFERENT, THEY ARE THE SAME!
Try these simple experiments yourself at home!

Magnets

- Energy cannot be created or destroyed, but it can change.

- Let us imagine we can accept the fact the electron is a standing wave of energy around the nucleus of an atom... BUT THERE IS MORE!

- This energy is moving, or pulsating. We refer to this movement as a spin.

- You may ask, What is the effect of this movement of energy? Well... in the real world, we see it as a magnetic field.
  • A magnetic field is generated by the electron rotating around its nucleus.
  • A magnetic field is also generated by the electron spinning inside of itself.
  (The Earth rotates around the sun every 365¼ days, and also on its axis once a day.)

- Usually the electron spinning inside of itself goes in a random direction – some spin one way, others spin the opposite way. The spins cancel themselves out, so the atom has no net magnetic field, and is neutral.

- BUT sometimes the electron spins are aligned, and when this happens, the atoms form a magnet. Magnets occur naturally. A rock called lodestone contains a mineral magnesia, named after the ancient town Magnesia, Greece.

WE LEARN ABOUT MAGNETISM AT A VERY EARLY AGE

What is an electron?

Let's Go Back in Time 200 Years...

■ **The magnetic field properties of electron flow were first discovered** by a remarkable young man named Michael Faraday who had no formal education, but worked for a book publisher. Because of his access to books, he loved to read and was fascinated by science. Back then very little was known about electricity. Although Faraday was never good at math, he loved to experiment and documented everything with great precision. What he discovered changed the whole world.

■ **He knew** that when you put a compass beside a copper wire, nothing unusual would happen and the needle would point towards the Earth's magnetic poles. However, if electricity flowed through the wire, the compass needle would immediately point at right angles to the wire. He took this observation one step further to discover:
   1) A wire placed next to a static magnet will move when an electric current flows through it. This was the beginning of the electric motor.
   2) Moving a magnet in and out of a coil of wire produces an electric current in the wire. This was the beginning of an electric generator.

■ **A new world** dawned because of Michael Faraday. Mechanical energy could be converted into electrical energy through a generator (think wind turbines) and electrical energy could be converted into mechanical energy via an electric motor.

■ **Other scientists and engineers of note include:**
Charles Augustin de Coulomb defined the electrostatic forces of attraction and repulsion. James Maxwell derived the mathematical equations that define the electromagnetic field properties. He brought the works of Faraday and Coulomb together. Nikola Tesla experimented with high voltage (millions of volts). Dmitri Mendeleev created the periodic table. Niels Bohr developed the first model of the atom. Alexander G. Bell invented the telephone. Thomas Edison invented the light bulb.

This hat is ridiculous

Photons

- You can't understand electricity and electrons without thinking about photons.

- A photon has **no mass and no charge**. An electron does have a mass and has a negative charge.

- One school of thought proposes that an electromagnetic field itself is produced by and is a **swarm of photons**. The interaction between two charged particles (i.e., between negatively charged electrons and/or between − electron and + nucleus) is the result of blasting photons back and forth between themselves. These photons contain the force information and are often called messenger particles. But wait… photons are much more.

- A photon is also "the smallest possible bundle of light". When we turn on a flashlight or point a laser we are emitting a stream of photons. They travel at 650 million miles per hour – the speed of light. Photons emitted from the Sun travel 93 million miles (150 million km) to Earth (taking 8 minutes). Everything we see is because of these photons hitting our eyes.

- Digital computers can also transmit data by firing photons from a laser over fibre optic or glass "wire". Such computers are called optical computers.

- **When an electron** moves from one energy state (cloud shape) to another, a packet of light called a photon is given off. You can actually see this as a **SPARK** if you ever get a static shock in the dark. A similar thing happens when a tungsten filament inside an incandescent light bulb gets heated.

- **Lightning** has been around forever. When atmospheric pressure builds inside a storm cloud, it forces the cloud to build up a positive (+) charge inside unevenly. When the charge gets too great, it will discharge to the negatively (-) charged ground/surface. This huge release of energy also emits photons which we see as a lightning flash.

37

What is an electron?

Atom Trivia

- There are 4 known forces in the universe: **Electromagnetism**, Gravity, Strong Nuclear Force (the Sun works by breaking this force), and Weak Nuclear Force (radioactive decay).

- The nucleus of an atom is a very busy place with as many as 19 particles such as protons, neutrons, neutrinos, tau, bosons, muons, gluons and quarks all contained inside.

- Much is still unknown about how these particles react with one another. We are building atom accelerators such as the new Hadron Super Collider in Europe, which tries to smash atoms together to answer some of these questions.

Everyone knows about gravity

- String theory tries to link all 4 of the forces of nature together. This is the **bees knees** of physics or the "Theory of Everything" that Einstein so desperately sought. Currently, Gravity does not abide by the same set of rules as do the other 3 forces. Many physicists thought this was odd. String theory postulates that all these small particles inside the atom are made up of even smaller (a trillion times smaller) bits of energy similar to a vibrating string. The theory, simply put, says that depending how the string vibrates, it could become any of these larger particles, which also accounts for gravity via the graviton particle. The mathematics that links all this together actually exists in 11 dimensions! The problem is that we cannot prove experimentally that string theory is real with our current technology.

- **The nucleus** of an atom is the most dense material known. A teaspoon of water weighs 1 gram. A teaspoon of nucleus would weigh 1 trillion kilograms. Recall that the atom is mostly space. It would take a lot of atoms stripped of their space to make a teaspoon of pure nucleus.

Everything *I* Need To Know About Electricity

- **99% of our Sun is made up of only 2 atoms.** Two hydrogen atoms smash together eventually forming a helium atom (thermonuclear fusion), and then 2 helium atoms smash together to form 4 hydrogen atoms (thermonuclear fission). Every atom smashing causes a tremendous nuclear explosion which releases energy in the form of light, heat and electromagnetic energy. Our Sun and all stars in the night sky have been doing this for billions of years already and will continue doing this for billions more to come.

- **Our planet contains a rotating molten iron (Fe) and nickel (Ni) core.** This movement induces an electrical current which produces a magnetic field around Earth. This magnetic field protects our planet from the deadly cosmic radiation. We would not be here if it was not for this magnetic field. A compass needle reacts to this field.

- There are only a few elements in the periodic table whose nucleus will react to an external magnetic field. Hydrogen is one. A hospital's MRI machine images the hydrogen protons in our body.

Only a few atoms (concentrations by mass) **make up almost everything!**

Name/Atomic #		Hydrogen/1	Helium/2	Carbon/6	Nitrogen/7	Oxygen/8
Symbol	Total	H	He	C	N	O
Sun	99%	74%	24%			< 1%
Universe*	99%	74%	24%	0.5%	0.1%	1.0%
Air (Breathable)	99%				78%	21%
Human Body	96%	10%		18%	3%	65%
Water (Ocean)	97%	11%				86%

* A large part of the universe is unknown and referred to as dark matter and energy

How can these 5 atoms make up almost everything ... including me!

39

What is an electron?

THIS MAY LOOK LIKE SCIENCE FICTION…

Everything I Need To Know About Electricity

BUT IN FACT IS BASED ON REALITY

Copper Atom

Concept based on *"Nature" Sept. 1999* Zou et al, Arizona State University

41

Chapter 3:

Computers are built from tiny switches called transistors.

Everything *I* Need To Know About Electricity

Forces Of Nature

- Electromagnetism is one of the 4 fundamental forces in nature along with gravity and the weak and strong nuclear forces. Electrostatic and magnetic forces are linked together to form electromagnetism. When you talk about electricity, you are always talking about electromagnetism. Recall that a change in electron flow always produces a magnetic field. Similarly, a change in magnetic field always produce an electron flow.

- Transistors, which are no more than on/off switches, work because of the electrostatic force. You can see this force by rubbing a balloon against your hair and sticking it to a wall. We can see electromagnetic forces at work by playing with a toy train.

Unlike Charges Attract Each Other (+ / -)

Like Charges Repel Each Other (+ / +) or (- / -)

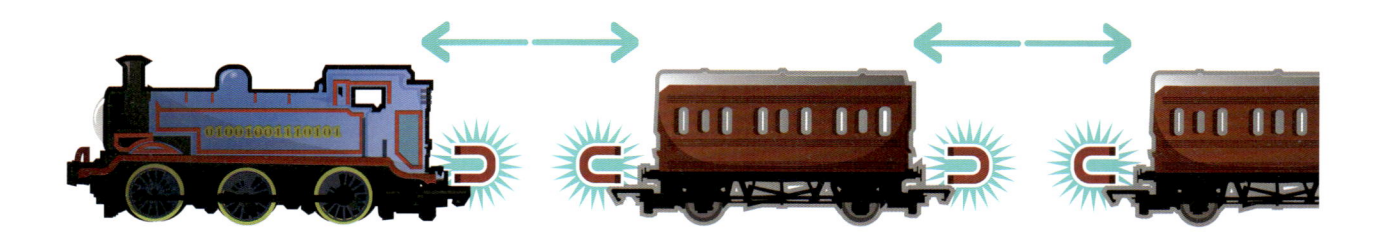

43

Computers are built from tiny switches called transistors.

Semiconductors

- **Computers today** are made up of billions of transistors which are made from a special family of atoms called **SEMICONDUCTORS.** Semiconductors will conduct electricity under certain conditions and will not conduct under others.

- **Three semiconductor** of importance are silicon, germanium and gallium-arsenide.

- **Commercial computers today** are made from mostly *silicon* which is found in sand and glass. Both boron and phosphorus are used as additives or dopants to silicon to form transistors.

Boron
P-Type Acceptor
missing electron relative to silicon

Silicon

Phosphorus
N-Type Donor
extra electron relative to silicon

Silicon Crystal Structure
equally spaced atoms
5.41 millionths of a metre apart

- **Did you know** that by adding only one donor atom into 100 million silicon atoms, the electrical conductivity increases by 24,100 times?

44

Everything *I* Need To Know About Electricity

- About 60 years ago, engineers at Bell Labs (USA) found a way of making an **ON/OFF SWITCH** called a **TRANSISTOR.** You can inject or "dope" silicon with neighbouring atoms that either have an extra electron called a donor (i.e., n-type such as phosphorus) or a missing electron, called an acceptor (i.e., p-type such as boron). This missing electron is referred to as a HOLE.

> **If you put a voltage on n-type silicon it becomes highly negatively charged.**
>
> **If you put a voltage on p-type silicon it becomes highly positively charged.**
>
> **If no voltage is present on either material, they become poor conductors or insulators.**

- All semiconductor atoms want to possess a filled outer valence shell. Let's imagine catching or passing a football. Depending on its doping, the silicon may be missing an electron/football or have an extra electron/football. If it receives a electron, it must get rid of an electron. The absence of a electron is called a "hole". When it receives an electron, the hole is filled. The atom losing its football becomes a hole and attracts another football. This creates an electron flow or hole flow, which are opposite. **This concept exists only in semiconductors.**

receiving electron   **creating hole**

- While a normal conductor is only concerned about the flow of electrons, semiconductors can conduct electricity by the flow of electrons or by the flow of holes.

45

Computers are built from tiny switches called transistors.

Transistors

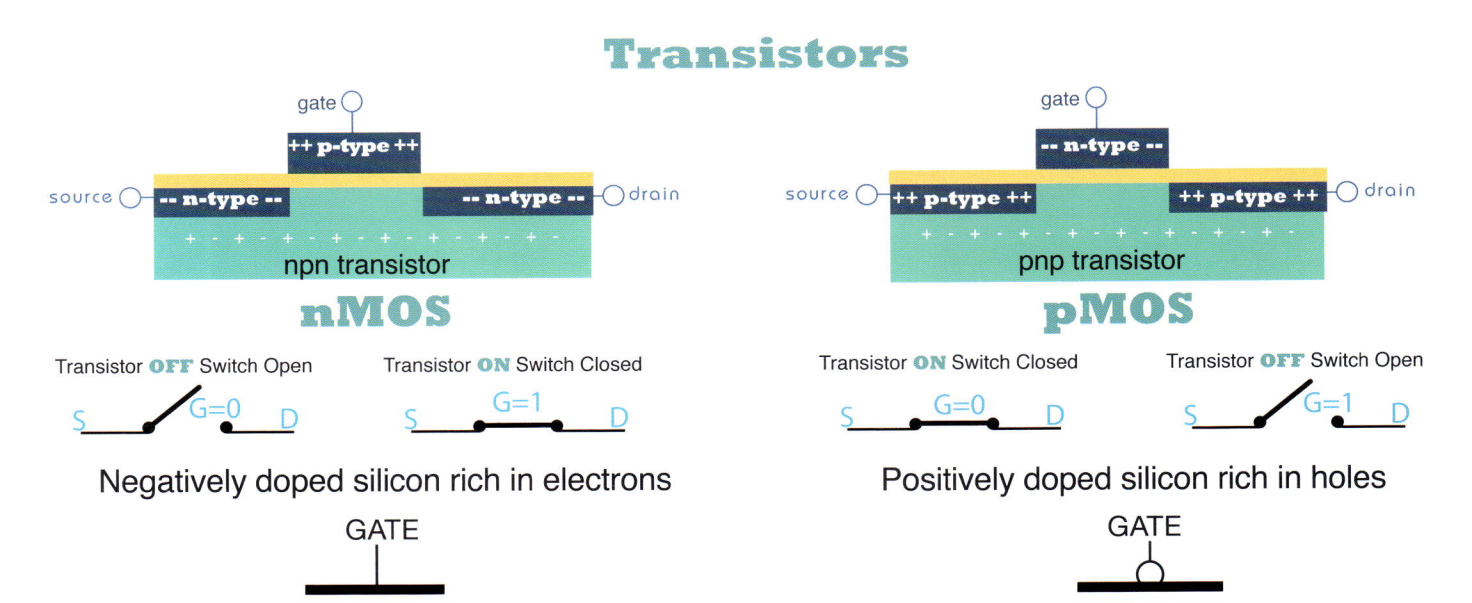

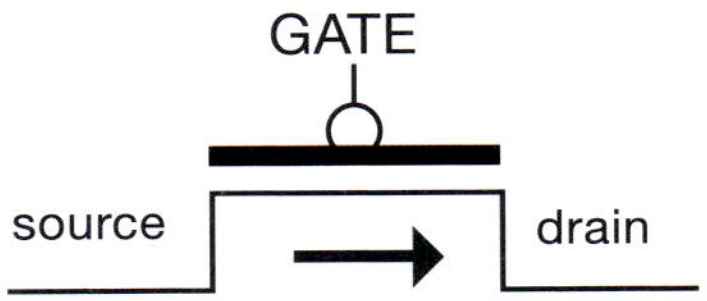

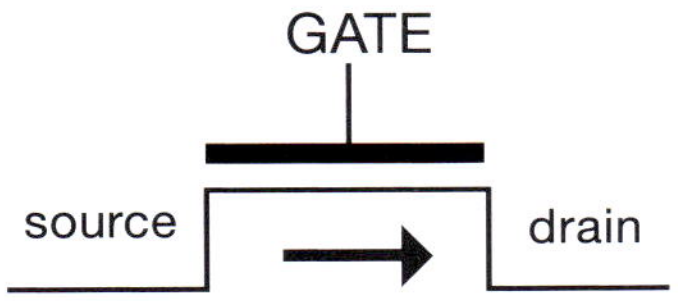

nMOS

npn transistor

Transistor **OFF** Switch Open — S G=0 D
Transistor **ON** Switch Closed — S G=1 D

Negatively doped silicon rich in electrons

GATE
source → drain

pMOS

pnp transistor

Transistor **ON** Switch Closed — S G=0 D
Transistor **OFF** Switch Open — S G=1 D

Positively doped silicon rich in holes

GATE
source → drain

The gate acts like a statically charged balloon and attracts all the majority carriers into the channel making a continuous conductor across the channel. These majority carriers could be either electrons or holes depending on how the transistor is made.

In computers, a transistor is just an ON/OFF SWITCH

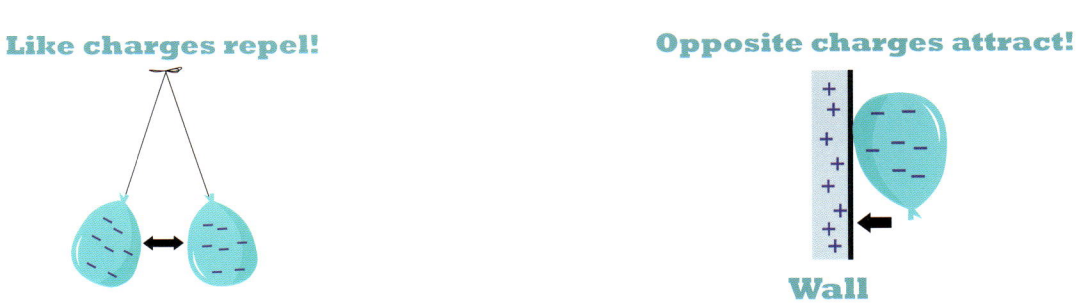

Like charges repel!

Opposite charges attract!

Wall

46

Everything *I* Need To Know About Electricity

Here is Another Look at How a Transistor Works

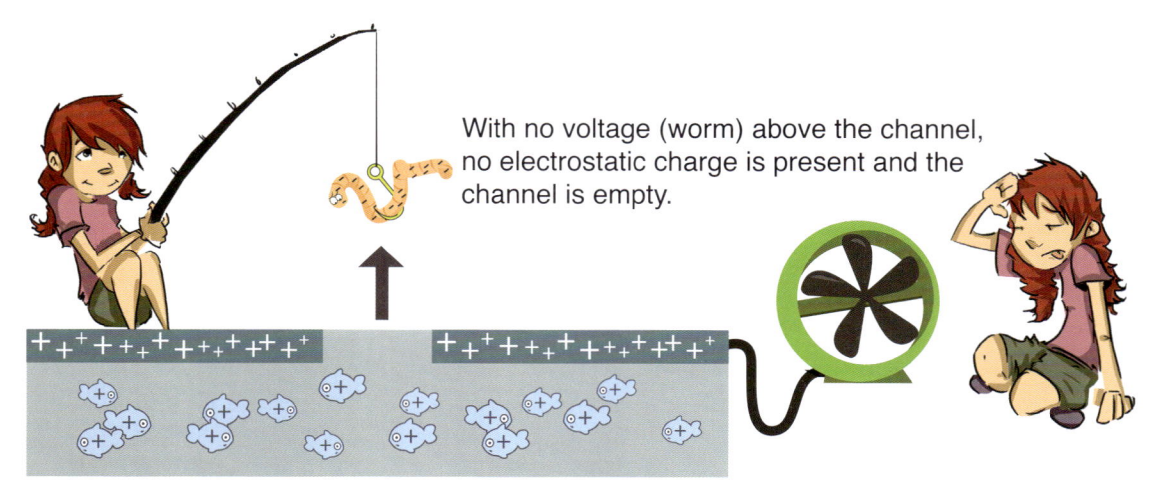

With no voltage (worm) above the channel, no electrostatic charge is present and the channel is empty.

THIS TRANSISTOR IS OFF, NO ELECTRON FLOW

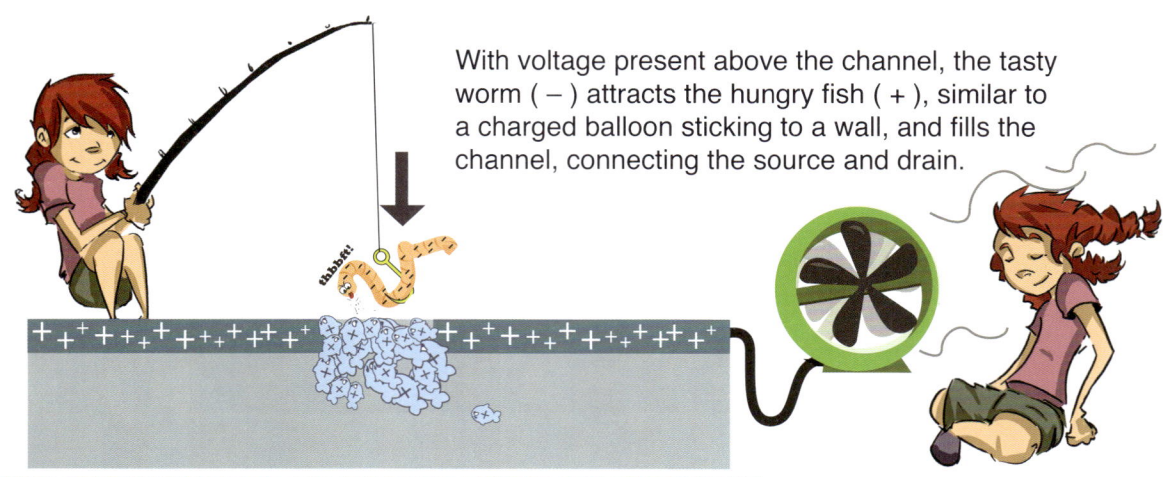

With voltage present above the channel, the tasty worm (−) attracts the hungry fish (+), similar to a charged balloon sticking to a wall, and fills the channel, connecting the source and drain.

THIS TRANSISTOR IS ON, ELECTRONS FLOW ACROSS IT

- This switch is call a Field Effect Transistor (FET). Depending on whether a voltage is present or not, an electrostatic field is produced above the gate which fills the channel and allows electricity to flow. **It is nothing more than an ON/OFF switch.**

47

Computers are built from tiny switches called transistors.

This is how a transistor looks on a silicon chip!

- **Transistors** are incredibly small. The channels shown are several billionths of a metre in width.

- **Video game consoles today** have a microprocessor containing ~ 300 million transistors. All this is on a piece of silicon the size of your thumbnail.

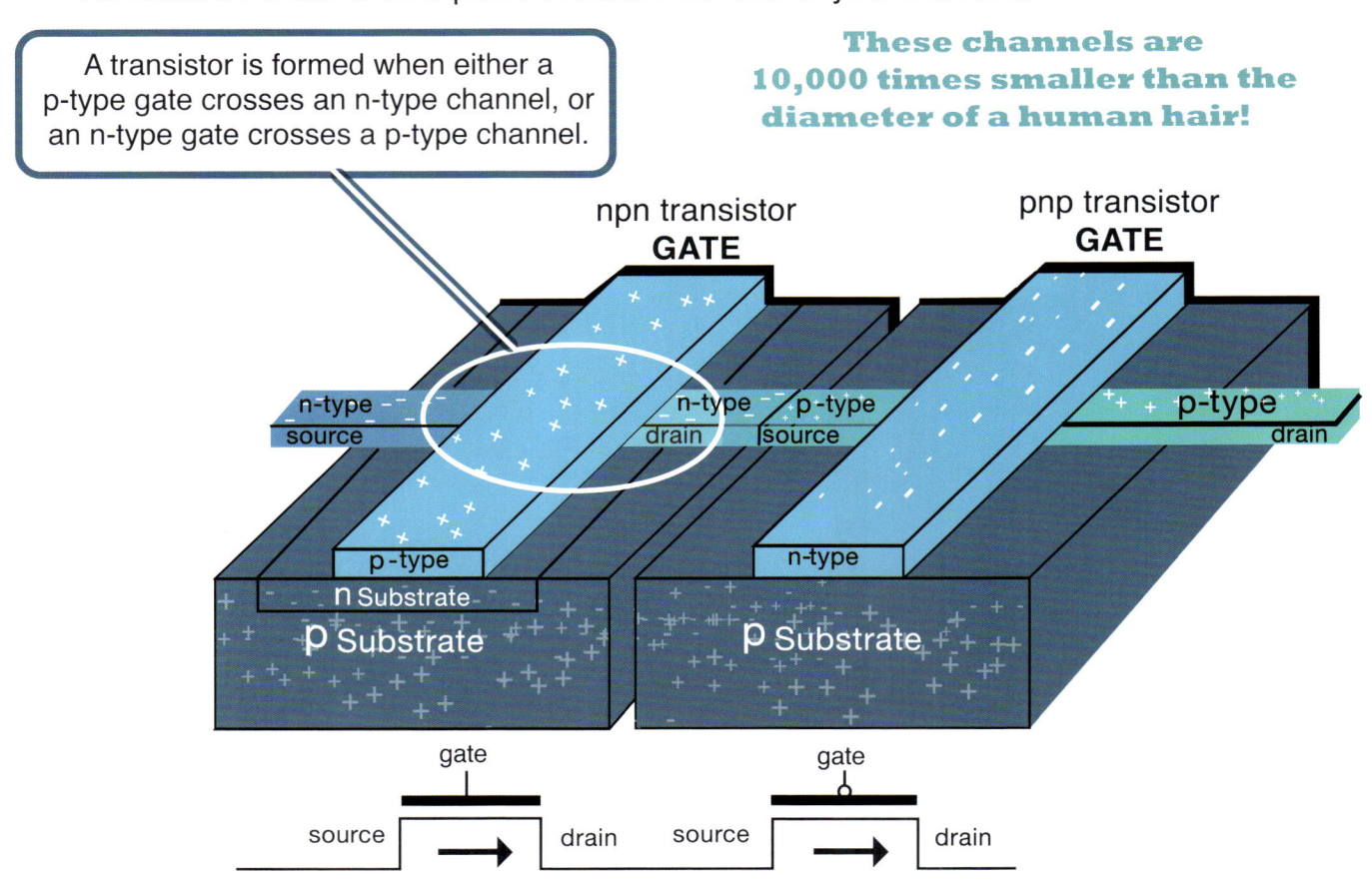

These channels are 10,000 times smaller than the diameter of a human hair!

A transistor is formed when either a p-type gate crosses an n-type channel, or an n-type gate crosses a p-type channel.

npn transistor **GATE**

pnp transistor **GATE**

n-type source | n-type drain | p-type source | p-type drain

p-type | n-type

n Substrate

p Substrate | p Substrate

gate — source → drain   gate — source → drain

- **This** is how you draw a CMOS (complementary metal oxide semiconductor) transistor.

- **Current flows** from Source to Drain ONLY if the gate is appropriately charged.

Everything *I* Need To Know About Electricity

All digital computers are made up of only 3 fundamental building blocks.

1) INVERTER GATE: made from 2 TRANSISTORS

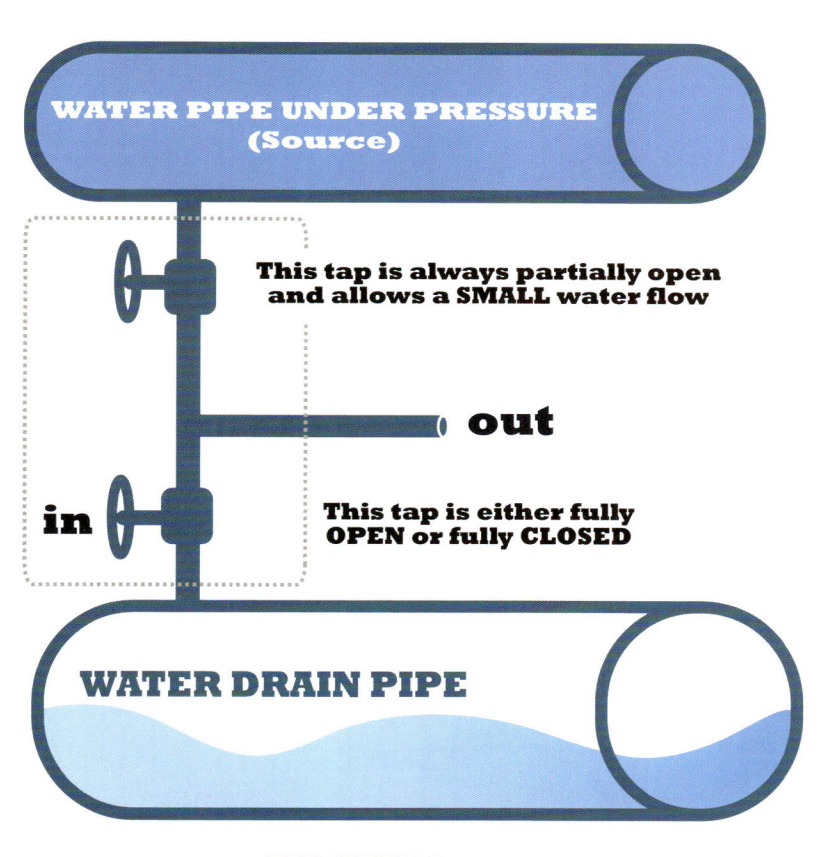

WATER PIPE UNDER PRESSURE (Source)

This tap is always partially open and allows a SMALL water flow

in

out

This tap is either fully OPEN or fully CLOSED

WATER DRAIN PIPE

Voltage Source Bus *

A special kind of transistor which is partially on. Allows a small current flow.

in

out

Ground Drain Bus *

*These buses are the voltage/electron pressure supply source and the destination drain for millions of transistors.

TRUTH TABLE

IN	OUT
Tap OFF	Water Flow ON
Tap ON	Water Flow OFF

INVERTER Gate

TRUTH TABLE

IN	OUT
1	0
0	1

SYMBOL

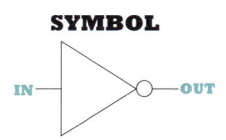

IN ──▷○── OUT

All logic gates are defined by their TRUTH TABLE which describes the relationship between inputs and outputs.

Computers are built from tiny switches called transistors.

2) NAND GATE: made from 3 TRANSISTORS
This is an example of a Series Circuit

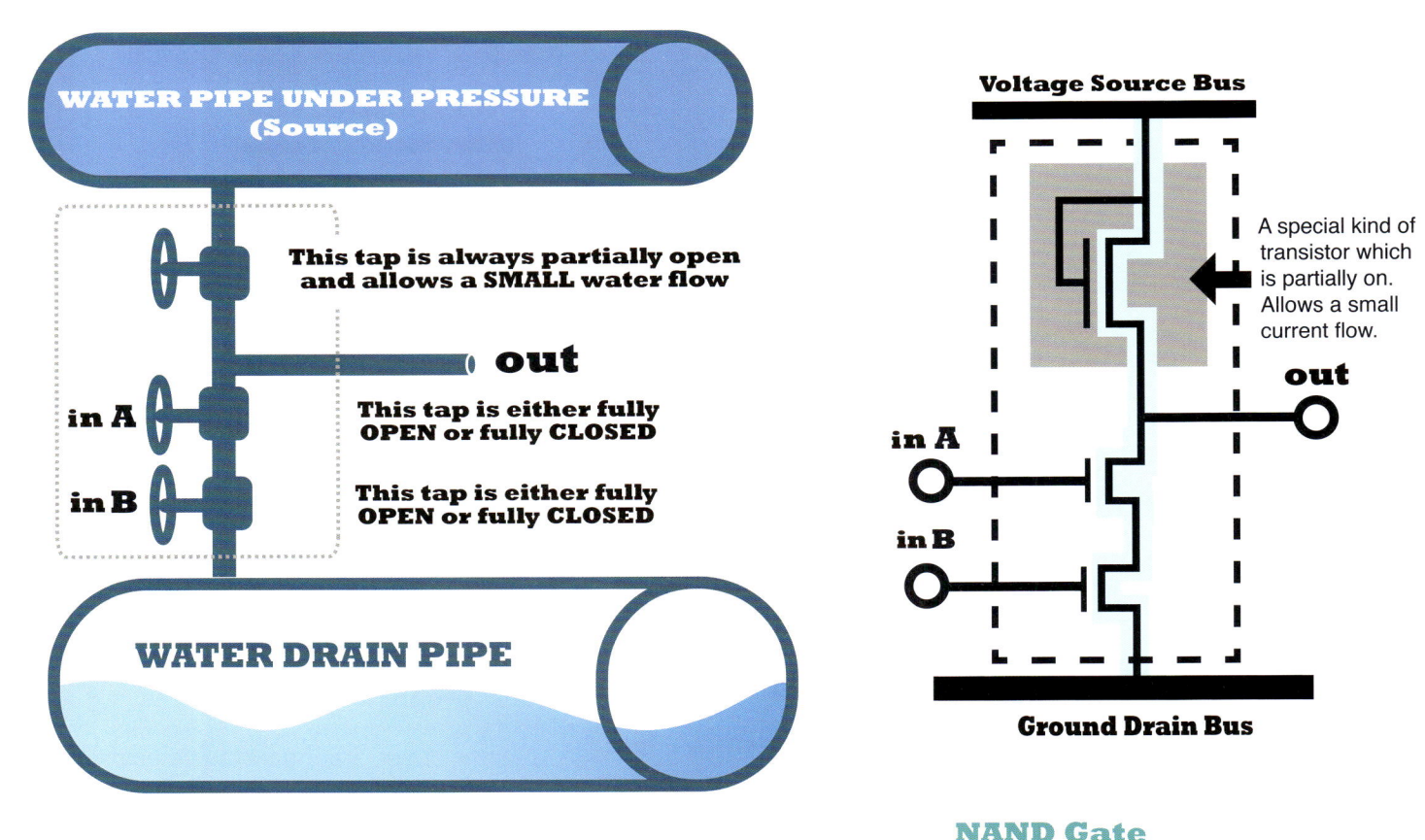

WATER PIPE UNDER PRESSURE (Source)

This tap is always partially open and allows a SMALL water flow

out

in A

This tap is either fully OPEN or fully CLOSED

in B

This tap is either fully OPEN or fully CLOSED

WATER DRAIN PIPE

Voltage Source Bus

A special kind of transistor which is partially on. Allows a small current flow.

out

in A

in B

Ground Drain Bus

NAND Gate

Truth Table

inA	inB	out
tap off	tap off	water flow on
tap off	tap on	water flow on
tap on	tap off	water flow on
tap on	tap on	water flow off

Truth Table

inA	inB	out
0	0	1
0	1	1
1	0	1
1	1	0

SYMBOL

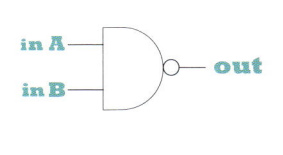

in A
in B
out

The NAND gate represents an "inverted AND" or Not-AND function. BOTH INPUT A **AND** B MUST BE VALID FOR THE OUTPUT TO BE INVALID

50

Everything *I* Need To Know About Electricity

3) NOR GATE: made from 3 TRANSISTORS
This is an example of a Parallel Circuit

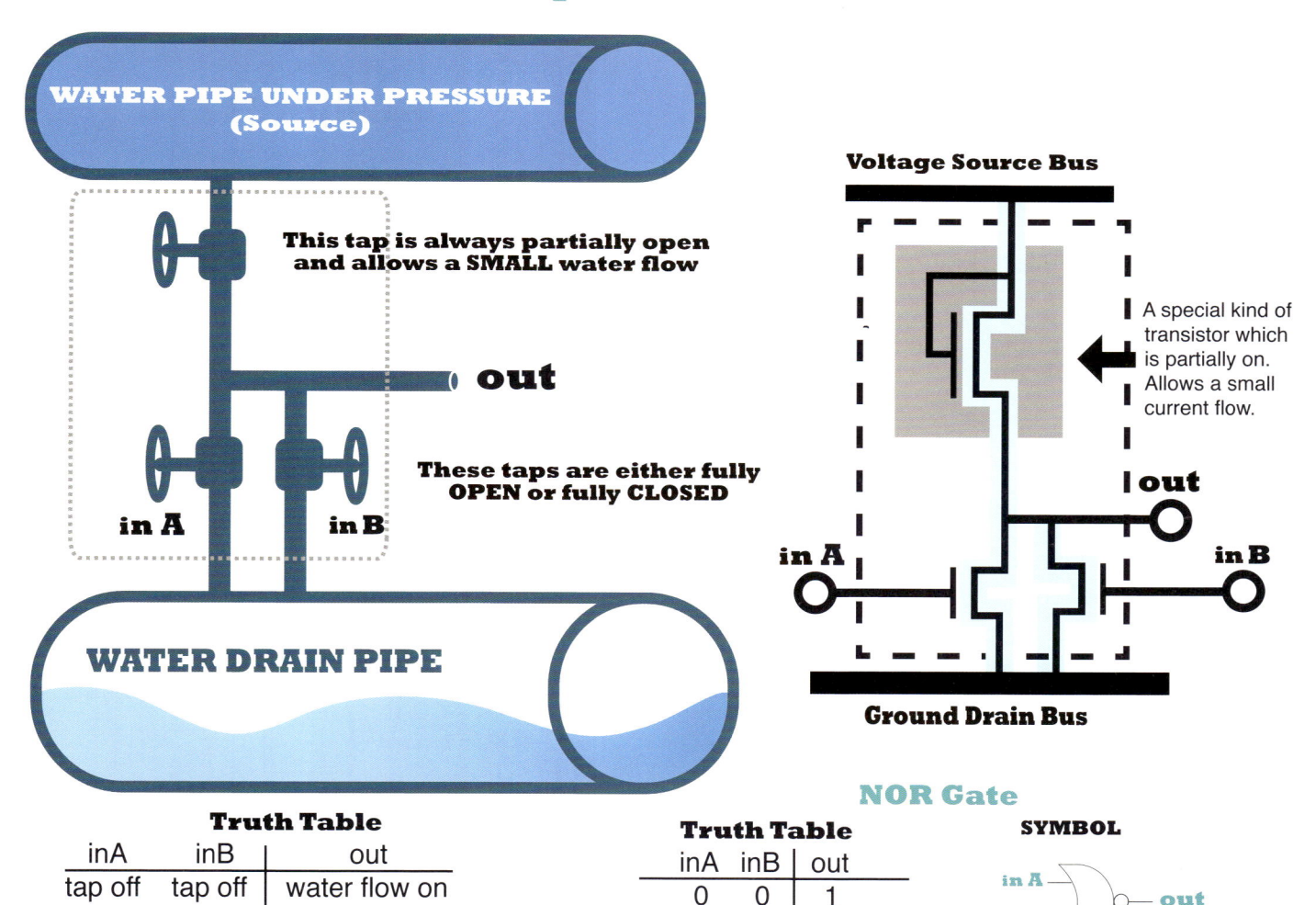

WATER PIPE UNDER PRESSURE (Source)

This tap is always partially open and allows a SMALL water flow

out

These taps are either fully OPEN or fully CLOSED

in A   in B

WATER DRAIN PIPE

Voltage Source Bus

A special kind of transistor which is partially on. Allows a small current flow.

out

in A   in B

Ground Drain Bus

Truth Table

inA	inB	out
tap off	tap off	water flow on
tap off	tap on	water flow off
tap on	tap off	water flow off
tap on	tap on	water flow off

NOR Gate

Truth Table

inA	inB	out
0	0	1
0	1	0
1	0	0
1	1	0

SYMBOL

in A
in B
out

- The NOR gate represents an "inverted OR" function which is a shortened Not-OR. EITHER INPUT A **OR** B MUST BE VALID FOR THE OUTPUT TO BE INVALID

51

Computers are built from tiny switches called transistors.

One Bit Memory Cell:
Built from 2 inverter gates containing a total of 6 transistors.

ONE BIT MEMORY CELL

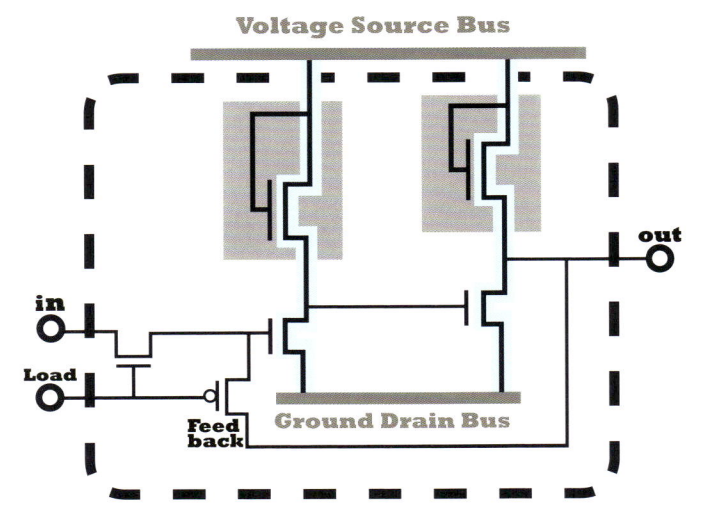

ONE BIT MEMORY CELL

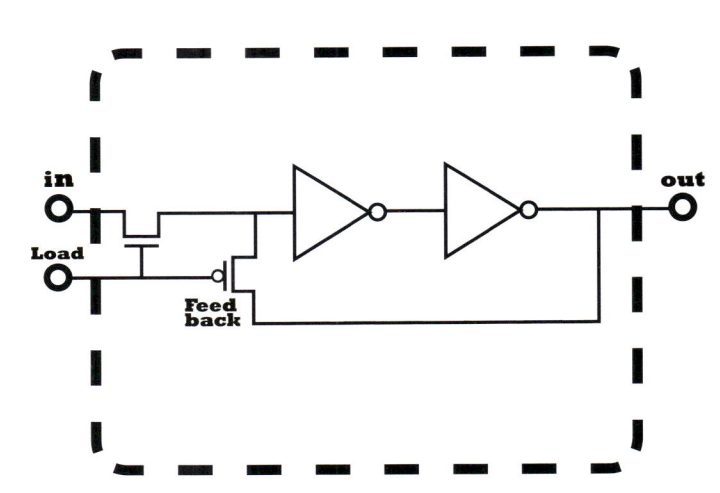

Truth Table

IN	LOAD	* Feedback	OUT
1	1	0	1
X	0	1	1
0	1	0	0
X	0	1	0

X= Don't care

* Feedback is for internal reference only. It is not part of the truth table, but is shown for clarity.

SYMBOL

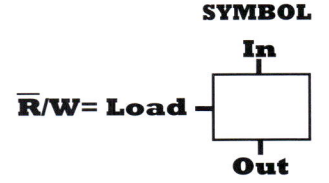

$\overline{R/W}$= Load

Often the term "load" is replaced with $\overline{R/W}$. If the input is digital "0" we are *Reading* the memory cell, if the input is digital 1, we are *Writing* or loading the memory cell. Note that $\overline{R/W}$ is connected to both nMOS and pMOS transistors. They act as transmission gates. A single signal can turn one on and the other off simultaneously, and vice versa.

52

Everything *I* Need To Know About Electricity

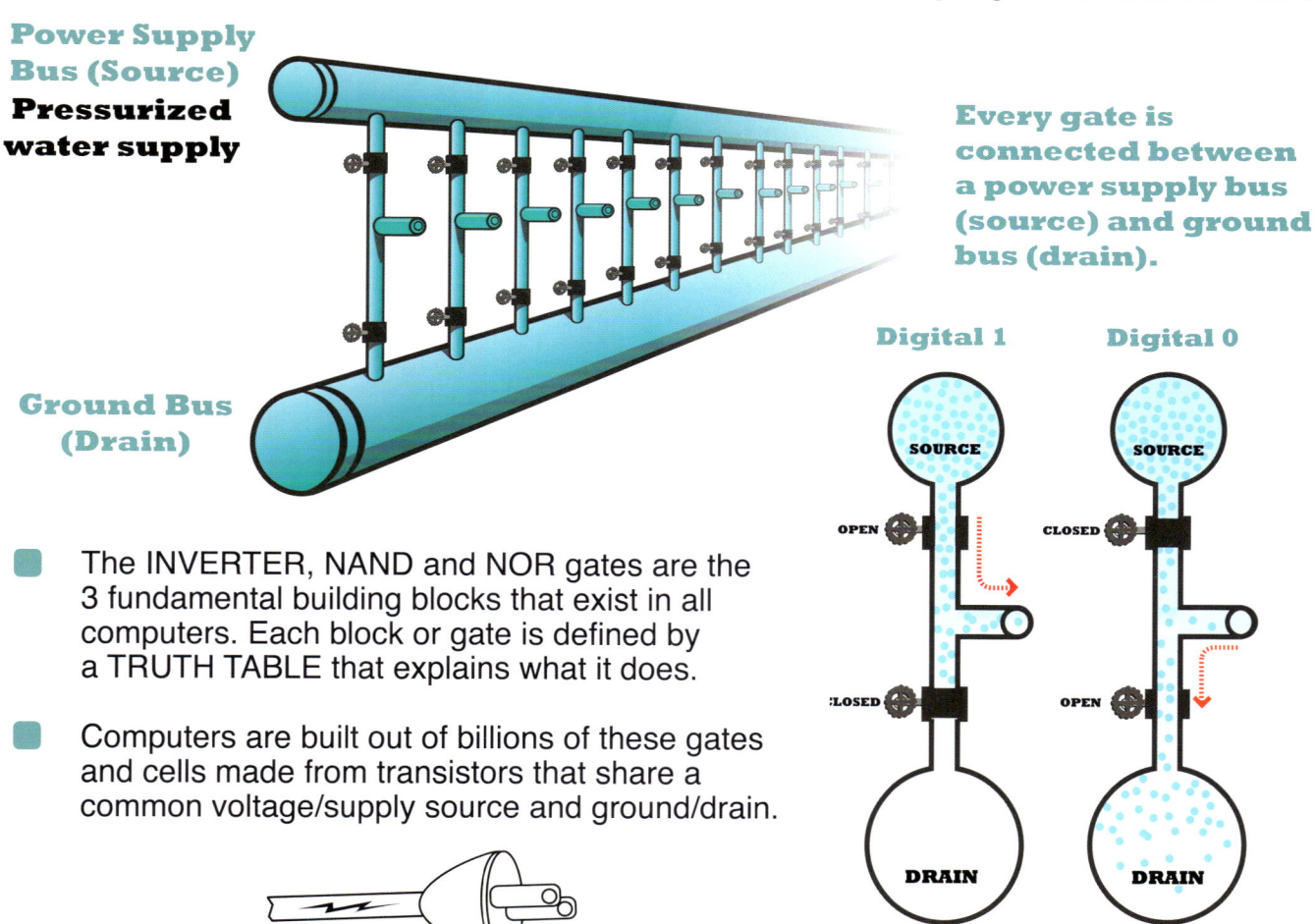

Power Supply Bus (Source)
Pressurized water supply

Ground Bus (Drain)

Every gate is connected between a power supply bus (source) and ground bus (drain).

Digital 1 — SOURCE, OPEN, CLOSED, DRAIN
Digital 0 — SOURCE, CLOSED, OPEN, DRAIN

- The INVERTER, NAND and NOR gates are the 3 fundamental building blocks that exist in all computers. Each block or gate is defined by a TRUTH TABLE that explains what it does.

- Computers are built out of billions of these gates and cells made from transistors that share a common voltage/supply source and ground/drain.

- All electrical plugs are exactly the same. One half of the plug represents a voltage/source supply, the other half is the ground/drain. Some plugs have a 3rd prong which is a duplicate ground/drain used for safety purposes. The voltage/source supply is 120 volts in North America and 230V almost everywhere else in the world.

Understanding electricity is Science. It is knowledge. Taking this knowledge and applying to do useful things is called Engineering! We can take a simple transistor and engineer complex machines called computers.

53

Chapter 4:

What does digital mean?

Everything *I* Need To Know About Electricity

One Bit Digital Memory Cell

One Bit Digital Memory Cell using Water

Depending which tap (or switch) is on, the hose can either be hard (digital 1) or soft (digital 0).

One Bit Silicon Digital Memory Cell using Transistors

Depending which transistor (or switch) is on, the wire can either have a voltage present (digital 1) or voltage absent (digital 0).

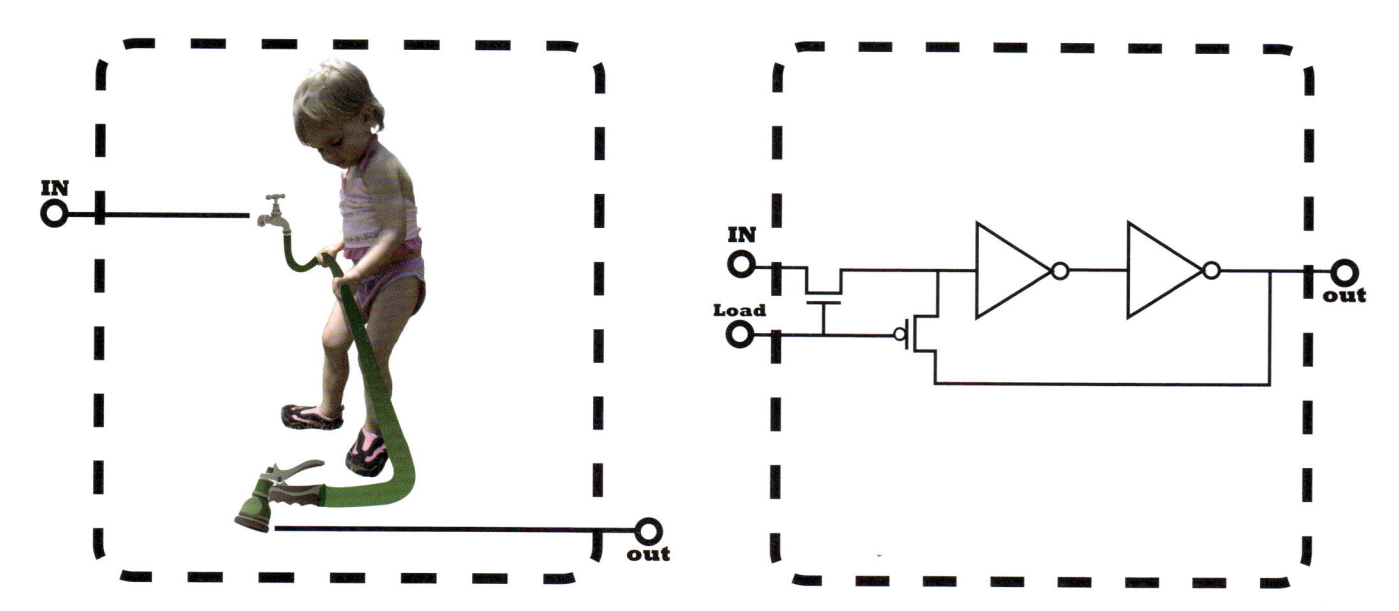

- Both electrical wire made out of silicon separated by transistors and a piece of water hose separated by taps can be viewed as one bit memory cells.

55

What does digital mean?

Digital means binary numbers

- **A binary number (a bit)** can have only two states, 0 or 1, just like a hose which can be **HARD or SOFT.**

- **Every number** known can be represented by an equivalent binary number. The following example shows four bits representing 16 distinct numbers, or states.

3 $2^3 = 8$	2 $2^2 = 4$	1 $2^1 = 2$	0 $2^0 = 1$	Bit Value = k Equivalent Value = 2^k
0	0	0	0	= 0 + 0 + 0 + 0 = **0**
0	0	0	1	= 0 + 0 + 0 + 1 = **1**
0	0	1	0	= 0 + 0 + 2 + 0 = **2**
0	0	1	1	= 0 + 0 + 2 + 1 = **3**
0	1	0	0	= 0 + 4 + 0 + 0 = **4**
0	1	0	1	= 0 + 4 + 0 + 1 = **5**
0	1	1	0	= 0 + 4 + 2 + 0 = **6**
0	1	1	1	= 0 + 4 + 2 + 1 = **7**
1	0	0	0	= 8 + 0 + 0 + 0 = **8**
1	0	0	1	= 8 + 0 + 0 + 1 = **9**
1	0	1	0	= 8 + 0 + 2 + 0 = **10**
1	0	1	1	= 8 + 0 + 2 + 1 = **11**
1	1	0	0	= 8 + 4 + 0 + 0 = **12**
1	1	0	1	= 8 + 4 + 0 + 1 = **13**
1	1	1	0	= 8 + 4 + 2 + 0 = **14**
1	1	1	1	= 8 + 4 + 2 + 1 = **15**

Try this at home!
Line 4 coins in a row similar to this table. Let each coin represent a binary value of HEADS(1) or TAILS(0)

Prove to yourself that you can define 16 unique states (0 to 15) by flipping them either as heads or tails.

How many unique states could you define with a row of 128 coins?

Everything *I* Need To Know About Electricity

ALL computers and the Internet communicate digitally using binary numbers which are voltage levels along a wire

Example:

5 V
0 V

256 128 64 32 16 8 4 2 1

0000 0001 0000 0101 = 256 + 4 + 1 = 261

01010100 01001000...01010100

*(There are **10** kinds of people in the world, those who understand binary, and those who don't)*

Number of bits or **Register Size**	Number of possible numbers **Distinct States (hard / soft)**
4 bit (a nibble)	2^4 = 16 *(see previous example, page 56)*
8 bit (a byte)	2^8 = 256
16 bit (a word)	2^{16} = 65,536
32 bit	2^{32} = 4,294,967,296 (4 Gigabit)
64 bit	2^{64} = 18,446,744,073,709,551,616 (18.4×10^{18})
128 bit	2^{128} = 340 trillion trillion trillion (340×10^{36})

What would a 256 bit or even a 512 bit encryption mean?

- **Rows** of one bit memory cells are grouped together to form registers which contain binary numbers and can convey huge amounts of information.

57

What does digital mean?

ASCII Symbol	Decimal Symbol	Binary Equivalent
A	65	01000001
B	66	01000010
C	67	01000011
D	68	01000100
E	69	01000101
F	70	01000110
G	71	01000111
H	72	01001000
I	73	01001001
J	74	01001010
K	75	01001011
L	76	01001100
M	77	01001101
N	78	01001110
O	79	01001111
P	80	01010000
Q	81	01010001
R	82	01010010
S	83	01010011
T	84	01010100
U	85	01010101
V	86	01010110
W	87	01010111
X	88	01011000
Y	89	01011001
Z	90	01011010
(space)	32	00100000
(period)	46	00101110

- **Look** at the keyboard on your computer. Every single key has a unique binary number associated with it.

- **These binary** numbers are called ASCII codes (American Standard Code for Information Interchange).

- **Eight** binary digits (think 8 water hoses, side by side, either hard or soft) are required for each letter of the alphabet. That seems like a lot. BUT IS IT? A standard dictionary has about 2,000 pages containing about 3,500 alphabet characters per page for a total of 7 million characters.

- **Did you know** that an ordinary blank CD, which you can buy for less than a candy bar, can hold 700 million bytes of data. Each byte contains 8 bits.

- **You** can store 100 books, comparable to a 2,000-page dictionary, on such a CD. Inexpensive memory sticks can store 1,000 similar sized books.

Everything I Need To Know About Electricity

When you text someone, you are sending ASCII binary codes
Example:

01001001	00100000	01001100	01001111	01010110	01000101	00100000
I	*space*	L	O	V	E	*space*

01000100	01001001	01000111	01001001	01010100	01000001	01001100
D	I	G	I	T	A	L

- Digital = Binary: It is the presence or absence of electron pressure between 2 transistors which is identical to the presence or absence of water pressure between 2 taps... *Is the hose hard/soft?*

- Everything, and I mean everything ... pictures, books, music ... can be represented digitally!

IT IS ALL DATA.

What does digital mean?

How does the digital world store music or speech?

- **Think** about a speech signal leaving a microphone or telephone. Your speech is contained in the resulting electrical ANALOG signal. The peaks and valleys of the signal waveform is analogous to the highs and lows in your voice.

- **Suppose** we had a camera and could take a series of pictures of this signal. Every snapshot of the signal is called a SAMPLE. We would measure the HEIGHT or SIGNAL STRENGTH of each sample and assign a NUMBER to it. Your speech would now be represented by a series of numbers represented in binary form.

- This process of converting a continuous analog waveform into a series of binary numbers is called **Analog-to-Digital (A to D) conversion**. Similarly, the reverse process of taking a series of binary digital numbers and reconstructing the original analog waveform is called **Digital-to-Analog (D to A) conversion**.

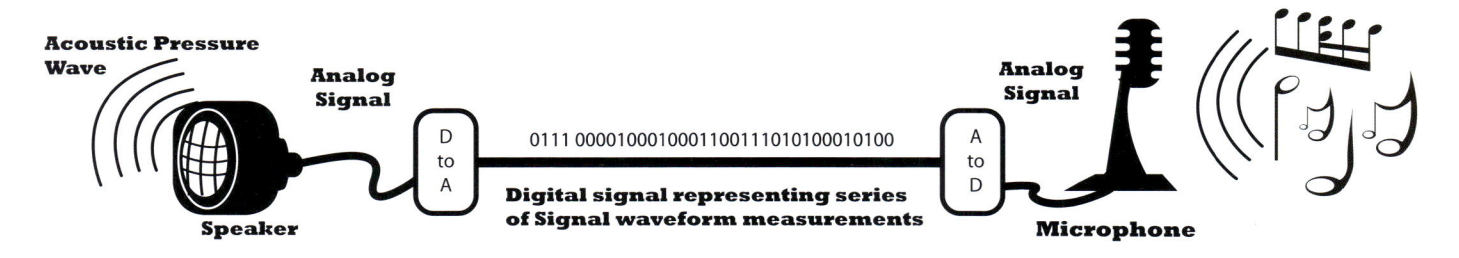

Acoustic Pressure Wave → Speaker ← **Analog Signal** ← D to A ← 0111 0000100010001100111010100010100 **Digital signal representing series of Signal waveform measurements** → A to D → **Analog Signal** → Microphone

When sending digital binary data, imagine riding an energy wave travelling at a billionth of a second per inch.

On a silicon chip, the transistors are so small and so close together, how long would the data take to travel one billionth of an inch?

What does digital mean?

How does the digital world store pictures or video?

PIXEL = an individual square of colour in a grid of squares that make up a picture

x100 zoom

x10 zoom

- **Whether** on your TV or in a photograph, pictures can be represented by an array of small dots called PIXELS. Each pixel will have a block of binary numbers associated with it. These numbers uniquely define each pixel's colour (red/green/blue), brightness and contrast.

- Each binary digit could be imagined as a small segment of wire between 2 transistors. This small segment could have an electron pressure/voltage present (digital 1) or absent (digital 0). This is similar to a hose between 2 taps which could be hard or soft.

- **A DVD in Blu-ray** format can hold 54 billion bytes (GB) of data. This is enough for about 2 hours of High Definition video.

Everything *I* Need To Know About Electricity

If you point a satellite dish at space you will hear static. We would call this digital 0. Any noise, whatever it is, could be considered digital 1. If this noise exists in a pattern, then we have a signal.

■ **The Cassini-Huygens spacecraft** travelled to SATURN and sent digital pictures over 770 million miles back to EARTH.

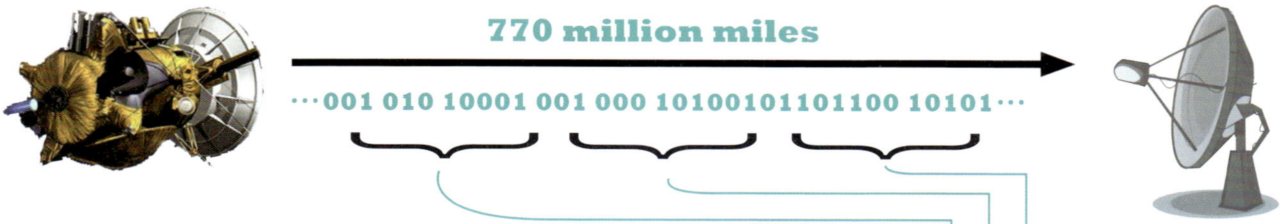

770 million miles

⋯001 010 10001 001 000 10100101101100 10101⋯

■ **A 2 mega pixel camera** captures a 1920 column x 1080 row = 2,073,600 pixel array. High Definition (HD) television updates this 2 mega pixel array 30 times a second.

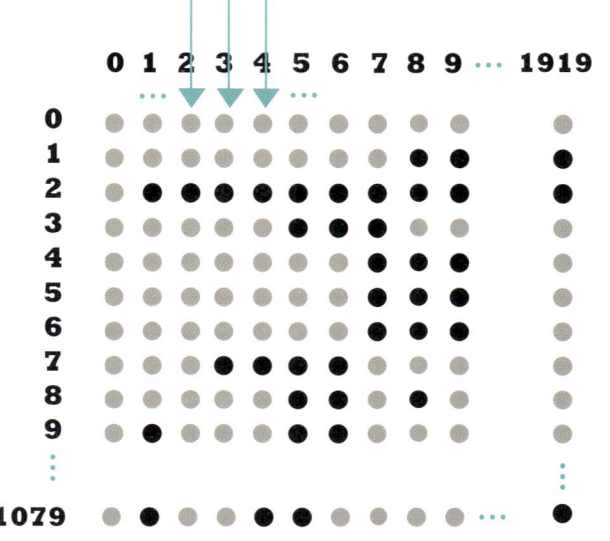

63

Greetings from planet Pemulak!

Lets examine today's CELL phones: Internet, video, photos, music, apps, GPS and don't forget speech. ALL DIGITAL ...travelling at the speed of light ...anywhere in the world ...and beyond??

What could you build with this knowledge?

Chapter 5:
A Different View of Time

WHAT IS A SECOND?
- SNAP YOUR FINGERS
- BLINK YOUR EYES

- **The fastest** you could press your video game controller or a piano key is about 3 times a second. Rarely can people do things faster than that.

- **WHAT DOES A SECOND MEAN TO A COMPUTER?** An ordinary computer you buy in a store today (3 GHz) moves DIGITAL DATA from location to location controlled by switches called transistors every 333 millionths of a second.

- **Now compare** this to a person doing a similar operation every second... It would take 100 years' worth of seconds to do what this computer could do in 1 second.

- **Engineers and scientists** today have successfully turned on and off a digital device a billion times faster than this. If a computer was built from this technology, it would take a person 4 billion years' worth of seconds to do what such a computer could do in 1 second.

- **Cyberspace** is the secret world inside computers which includes the Internet. It exists because of the flow of electrons that are configured to represent specific binary values for a very small period of time on a very small piece of silicon wire.

- **Data** representing speech, video, music, books – **INFORMATION** – flows at incredible speed approaching the speed of light or at 670 million miles per hour. A second is an eternity in cyberspace.

A Different View of Time

- Today incredibly fast and powerful computers are commonplace. All this came about recently within the last 50 years.

- Today, a bit can be contained in wires several hundred atoms wide and several hundred atoms deep containing about 50,000 electrons. Technology is making this number smaller and smaller and eventually, within the near future, 1 bit might be represented by only 1 electron.

- In the recent past, computers were termed "single core" which meant a single processor or engine built on silicon, often termed "hardware". Recently, the terms "dual core" and "quad core" became common. How about a single chip containing 100 cores, with each processing 64 bits of data every 1.5 billionths of a second, supported by 1 trillion bytes of data, all for $50! Welcome to the 21st century.

- The programs that run these machines are called "software". Another name for a program is an application or an APP. Programs are written in human time which specifies the routing paths of the data. Programs define the rules which the data abides to.

- A program consisting of hundreds or thousands of lines of code or specific instructions, taking months or years to write and verify, could be executed in a blink of an eye.

- An example of a software program is the spell check program that runs on your computer. It compares each typed word to a dictionary, identifies words that do not match and offers options that could be what you want.

Everything *I* Need To Know About Electricity

Let's do a Mini Review:

- Playing with a garden hose or Super Soaker water gun can help you understand the basics of electron pressure and flow called voltage and current. Squeeze a garden hose while pressing the nozzle trigger. Feel the hose get hard and soft. This fundamental concept is the basis of all digital computers except it is happening a billion times faster and a billion times smaller.

- All bonding between atoms, which are mostly space, is a result of the interaction between the outermost unfilled valence electrons. A truly remarkable thing is that all life (Biology) and matter (Chemistry) as we know it exists because of the bonding of these outermost valence electrons which all abide by the laws of Physics.

- The basis of electricity in a conductor is the movement of free electrons that exist in an atom's outer unfilled valence orbit when a voltage or pressure is present.

- Electrons are standing waves of energy around the nucleus of an atom which are contained in specific cloud shapes. When they move, a magnetic field is produced.

- The digital world today exists because of our ability to measure and assign a number to any electrical signal which can be captured, stored, manipulated and reconstructed. This applies to all information or data in all its forms.

Digital 1 / Digital 0 = Hose hard / Hose soft = Voltage present / Voltage absent = Laser ON / Laser OFF

69

Closing Remarks

Imagine that you are sitting in a chair singing. Pretend you are the nucleus of an atom. The song you're singing could represent energy and fill a peculiar shaped room that extends 200 miles. Parts of your song extend past your room and may be heard by another person singing a different song. Your two songs sound so beautiful together that they join together and you form a duet, or a trio, a quartet or a choir. This concert could be the basis for all matter in the universe.

I remember when the term Gigabyte (billion/10^9) was unheard of. Now the term Terabyte (trillion/10^{12}) is becoming common. Soon Peta (10^{15}), Exa (10^{18}), Zetta (10^{21}) and Yotta (trillion trillion/10^{24}) will become commonplace. What could you do with a billion 512 bit cores, each working at a trillionth (pico/10^{-12}) of a second, each accessing unlimited memory? This is not science fiction – **all this will all come! ... and we will surpass this!**

What can you do with this knowledge and power which did not exist 50 years ago?

What does it take to turn an "I don't understand" into "I get it!" ?
What does it take to turn a NO into a YES?

I have just scratched the surface and opened the door a crack into the fascinating world of physics, chemistry and engineering to describe the concepts of electricity.
It is as much an art as it is anything!

You need imagination, curiosity, an open mind, a willingness to take risks, and above all *passion*.

Out of passion and imagination will come the thirst to understand.

Everyone faces problems that appear insolvable. You are not alone. When the challenge is the hardest and when everyone else is shaking their heads, find it in yourself to say:

LET'S GO!

thbbft!

END

END